AT ODDS

Tim,

God Bless You as You
Serve our Lord Jesus!

Soli deo Gloria!

Pastor Tom

Phil. 2:13

THOMAS CLOTHIER

AT ODDS

God's Development of Leaders through Conflict

TATE PUBLISHING
AND ENTERPRISES, LLC

Published by Tate Publishing & Enterprises, LLC
127 E. Trade Center Terrace | Mustang, Oklahoma 73064 USA
1.888.361.9473 | www.tatepublishing.com

Tate Publishing is committed to excellence in the publishing industry. The company reflects the philosophy established by the founders, based on Psalm 68:11,
"The Lord gave the word and great was the company of those who published it."

Cover design by Allen Jomoc
Interior design by Jomar Ouano

Published in the United States of America

ISBN: 978-1-62510-211-9
1. Religion / Christian Church / Leadership
2. Religion / Christian Church / Growth
13.04.30

Now to him who is able to do far more abundantly than all that we ask or think, according to the power at work within us, to him be glory in the church and in Christ Jesus throughout all generations, forever and ever. Amen.

—Ephesians 3:20–21, ESV

To Him who continues to do abundantly more than I can ever ask or think as He powerfully works within me. *Soli Deo Gloria.*

CONTENTS

Preface 9

1. A Leader and Conflict 11
2. The Theological and Biblical Issues of Conflict: Old Testament Examples 23
3. The Theological and Biblical Issues of Conflict: New Testament Examples 61
4. Profiles in Conflict: Job's Unwavering Trust in God's Character 87
5. Profiles in Conflict: Moses' Endurance by God's Direction 95
6. Profiles in Conflict: Joseph's Confidence in God's Care 105
7. Profiles in Conflict: David's Heartfelt Commitment to Uphold God's Glory! 125
8. Theoretical Foundations and Theological Conclusions Concerning Conflict 147
9. The Storm Clouds Gather 169
10. The Trial's Full Fury 175
11. Joy in the Trial 179

12. The Aftermath of the Trial 185
13. Pastors' Responses to Conflict Survey 195
14. Implementing Strategies and Goals 209

Bibliography 223

PREFACE

As I was preparing to enter Detroit Bible College in the fall of 1977, I was greatly encouraged by a guest speaker who filled the pulpit at the church my wife and I were attending and serving the Lord. He counseled that as the Lord would begin to use me in the ministry, it would be easy to begin thinking that it was I alone doing the work and therefore worthy of the praise and thanks I might receive.

He continued by stating that I should always remember that it would be, and always would be, God working through me for His glory. Soon after, I came upon Philippians 2:12–13, which soon would become my life's vision: "Therefore, my beloved, as you have always obeyed, so now, not only as in my presence but much more in my absence, work out your own salvation with fear and trembling, for it is God who works in you, both to will and to work for his good pleasure."

This book is a work that God has done through this servant. His slave! All believers will encounter trials and especially those called to be leaders. It is through those conflicts that God develops leaders to become better leaders for the kingdom and for His glory. I pray that this book will help all who read it to understand that.

My heartfelt thanks and appreciation is extended to many who have made this work a reality. My editor and colleague, Dennis Hensley, patiently listened to my thoughts and vision for this book over pie and coffee. He pushed and prodded, encouraged and explained. He continually believed that this book contained a message the church in particular and leaders in general needed to hear. Thank you, Dennis.

Thanks to my church family and friends, whether near or far. I thank my God in every remembrance of you. To my wife, Diana, who never wavers in her love for the Lord and for me. For my family, who are havens of grace in the midst of the turbulence of life. To my publishers who caught the value and God originated vision of a pastor from northeast Indiana.

Finally, to my Lord and Savior Jesus Christ! *Soli deo Gloria!*

CHAPTER ONE

A Leader and Conflict

I am a leader. I am a person of influence. So are you.

I serve the Lord as a pastor. You may be a Sunday school teacher, a youth sponsor, an elder in your church, or a deacon. You may own your own business, work in an office, teach in a school, or serve in a local hospital. You may serve as a police officer or in a local, state, or federal government position. Regardless of your title or responsibilities, you influence those around you. You are a leader!

Leaders face many challenges. That is why they're leaders. However, the greatest test of leadership will occur in conflict. God has called me to pastoral ministry. God has also permitted conflict and trials to occur in my pastoral ministry. I neither sought nor desired these conflicts. However, God used these times of testing to make me the godly leader He desires. The same is true for you. I have come to believe that conflict is an indispensable tool God uses to develop godly leadership.

The church where I currently pastor has risen from the smoldering embers of a "firestorm," which engulfed its ministries, its congregation, and my family several years ago. Unfounded accusations, gossip, manipulation, disobedience to church leadership, and a demonic influence consumed the church during those days. People were hurt, several families left the church, and I was mandated to take a leave of absence wherein I relinquished all ministry responsibilities. The church leadership prohibited me from officiating scheduled weddings, funerals, or having any pastoral involvement with anyone from the congregation. My family and I became isolated.

I often feared I would never be able to return to the ministry. What else could I do? Where would my family and I go? Our church, and its surrounding community, had become our home, but in my mind, I was damaged goods. I retreated and hid in the sanctuary of my home.

However, through professional and godly mediation, ongoing education and prayer, eventually, the church in general and I in particular arose from the fires of conflict into godly leadership which continually strives to glorify God. It was not easy, but the Lord continues to bring healing into my life, my family, and the congregation.

God has given me the privilege of being involved in some facet of pastoral ministry for thirty-plus years. He has chosen to use me as a Christian education pastor, youth pastor, and presently, as a senior pastor. During that time, the Lord has taught me that pastoral ministry remains a vital component to the overall function of the local church. Every pastor is a leader. He may be effective or ineffective, but he is a leader.

I have learned that conflict is an often unwelcome companion in pastoral ministry, but something that God can use to develop godly leaders. As one author has written, "God allows conflicts in order to humble us, test us, and create spiritual growth within us. Christians as well as non-Christians have conflicts; the difference is in the way we [believers] handle them." It is important for leaders to realize that it is not sinful to have conflict; it is only sinful when conflict is not handled in a biblical manner and the leader learns nothing from the conflict.

Many authors have written significant and helpful books regarding the topic of church conflict. Still others have written volumes on leadership. I have many of them in my office. However, whereas church conflict will be discussed, the purpose of this book is not primarily to study church conflict, but rather, it is to understand God's rationale for using conflict to develop godly leadership. This book not only will provide leaders a perspective concerning their own past conflicts, but it will also provide a primer for preparing for conflicts yet to come.

All ministries must be built upon obedience to biblical truth. To do so is to build one's life upon a solid rock. To do otherwise is to build one's life upon the sand. The decisive moment occurs when troubles come. As Jesus spoke in the Sermon on the Mount, the house (life) built on the rock will not fall. "And the rain fell, and the floods came, and the winds blew and beat on that house, but it did not fall, because it had been founded on the rock" (Matthew 7:25, ESV). While the house (life) built on the sand will fall. "And the rain fell, and the floods came, and the winds blew and beat against that house, and it fell, and great was the fall of it" (Matthew 7:27, ESV). As Pastor John Piper writes:

> The afflictions of John Bunyan gave us *The Pilgrim's Progress.* The afflictions of William Cowper gave us *There is a Fountain Filled with Blood* and *God Moves in a Mysterious Way.* And the afflictions of David Brainerd gave us a published *Diary* that has mobilized more missionaries than any other similar work. The furnace of suffering brought forth the gold of guidance and inspiration for living the Christian life, worshipping the Christian God, and spreading the Christian gospel. (Piper, 19)

This book examines the biblical theme of God's use of conflict to develop men and women to become the leaders He desires. This is taught implicitly, and explicitly, throughout the Old and New Testaments.

At the outset, clear definitions for the terms leadership and conflict are absolutely necessary for a correct understanding of how God chooses to develop leadership through conflict. Therefore, what is leadership?

Leadership expert, and former pastor, John Maxwell explains that "leadership is influence." That's it. Nothing more; nothing less! My favorite leadership proverb is "He who thinketh he leadeth and hath no one following him is only taking a walk" (Maxwell, 1).

What makes a godly leader?

Godly leadership is being a person of character. Character is morality and possessing a good reputation. A leader may be uniquely qualified with multiple degrees, supremely gifted with a dynamic personality, and ably talented as a communicator, but if he lacks a strong, moral character, his ministry or career will be superficial and inconsequential at best and damaging at worst. In this culture where "image is everything," the leader must be a person of moral substance. A leader whose character is a mile wide, but an inch deep, is not sufficient for the task at hand.

Concerning a leader's character Pastor Charles Haddon Spurgeon wrote, "Let us aspire to saintliness of spirit and character. I am persuaded that the greatest power we can get over our fellow men is the power which comes of consecration and holiness" (Michael, 75). Spurgeon believed that a leader must evidence an uncompromising standard of character.

Two definitive biblical passages focusing on a leader's character are found in 1 Timothy 3:1–7 (ESV) and Titus 1:5–9 (ESV). Both passages contain directives specifically regarding a pastor's responsibilities, but the vast majority of qualifications focus on what a pastor must be: a man of godly character. These qualities must not only be found in the godly leader but also continually developed by the leader cooperating with the Lord. These qualities include being:

- above reproach (1 Timothy 3:2; Titus 1:6, ESV). There must be no valid accusation of wrongdoing made against a pastor.
- the husband of one wife (1 Timothy 3:2; Titus 1:6, ESV). This literally means a one-woman man. He does not have a roving eye. He guards what he sees.
- sober minded (1 Timothy 3:2; Titus 1:7, ESV). This literally means "wineless." As a leader, he must possess the ability to think clearly. He abstains from the clouding influence of alcohol.
- self-controlled (1 Timothy 3:2; Titus 1:8, ESV). This refers to a disciplined individual. He is serious about spiritual matters.
- respectable (1 Timothy 3:2, ESV). This means "orderly." He does not lead a chaotic life.
- hospitable (1 Timothy 3:2; Titus 1:8, ESV). He is to be a lover of strangers. He must demonstrate a willingness to help and assist people.
- able to teach (1 Timothy 3:2, ESV). The preaching and teaching of God's word is a pastor's primary responsibility. This is the one of two qualifications alluding to the pastor's job.
- not a drunkard (1 Timothy 3:3; Titus 1:7, ESV). The pastor must not have a reputation as a drinker or drunkard.
- not violent (1 Timothy 3:3; Titus 1:7, ESV). This literally means "not a giver of blows." He cannot be a violent man.

- gentle (1 Timothy 3:3, ESV). He must demonstrate patience and understanding.
- not quarrelsome (1 Timothy 3:3, ESV). He is reluctant to fight.
- not a lover of money (1 Timothy 3:3; Titus 1:7, ESV). He must not be in the ministry for money. The pastor must not focus on wanting something more than what he has and, at the same time, resenting those who have what he does not have.
- manages his own household well (1 Timothy 3:4–5, ESV). He is to have an orderly home. This refers to family relationships.
- must not be a recent convert (1 Timothy 3:6, ESV). A pastor cannot be a novice.
- must be well thought of by outsiders (1 Timothy 3:7, ESV). He must have an impeccable reputation in the non-Christian community.
- not self-willed (Titus 1:7). He focuses on God's will.
- lover of good (Titus 1:8, ESV). He must have affection for that which is intrinsically and morally good.
- upright (Titus 1:8, ESV). The pastor evidences behavior which is proper.
- holy (Titus 1:8, ESV). He is to be set apart from sin's control and is controlled by God.
- holding firm to the trustworthy word (Titus 1:9, ESV). This is the second occurrence reflecting a pastor's job responsibility. The pastor is to teach and be committed to sound biblical doctrine.

As a pastor, I am to be a godly leader. This is true because a pastor is in a position of influence. Beyond the title, a pastor uniquely possesses the responsibility to influence God's people with God's truth resulting in godliness. With that God-ordained influence, a pastor must set forth an example of godly character which will glorify God while at the same time resonating with the congregation he serves.

So it is with any believer. I am a Christian who strives to be a godly leader. Your sphere of influence may be a carpool, an office, a construction site, or a classroom. Regardless of who you are, your influence as a leader is significant. People are following your lead.

However, leadership is not just about what we are but also what we do. Leadership is also being a person of integrity. Integrity is "moral uprightness; honesty" (Oxford, 422). Integrity means "wholeness; soundness" (Oxford, 422). While character focuses on what a leader is, integrity involves what a leader does. It is the leader's conduct.

Integrity is being consistent with biblical convictions. For a pastor, this is essential for effective leadership. People may not necessarily agree with a pastor's biblical convictions, but they will respect him for holding to his biblical convictions, regardless of the consequences. For the pastor, or any leader, to do otherwise is hypocrisy.

Pastor Charles H. Spurgeon also believed that pastors must be men of integrity and that it was essential in the work of the ministry. In a letter to young pastors, he wrote:

> Dear brethren, we must acquire certain moral facilities and habits, as well as put aside their opposites. He will never do much for God who has not integrity of spirit. If we be guided by policy, if there be any mode of action for us but that which is straightforward, we shall make shipwreck before long. Resolve, dear brethren, that you can be poor, that you can be despised, that you can lose life itself, but

rather being attacked by or attacking the person who holds a different opinion.

The Scriptures contain two words for conflict: "ἀγών" (*agon*) and "ἄθλησις" (*athlesis*). The word "agon" has several meanings: (1) a place of assembly, (2) a contest of athletes. This idea is used metaphorically in referring to the Christian life as a fight and a race, and (3) the spiritual conflict of the soul, which is often the result of an accompanying outward conflict. This definition is explicitly taught in the New Testament, and from it, we derive the English word "agony."

Conflict involves a "striving for the goal." It involves exertion and a concentrating of one's forces. Little reference is made to antagonists, but obstacles and dangers have to be faced. Martyrdom is the final conflict.

In Philippians 1:29–30 (ESV), the Apostle Paul explained that conflict is a part of being a Christian. He shared that for the Christian, suffering was to be expected. He expressed the same thought in his other epistles. The content of his writing reflected the experiences of his life and God's truth.

Paul expressed an inner conflict to the Colossians in his desire to encourage them. He stated, "What a great conflict I have for you and those in Laodicea, and for as many as have not seen my face in the flesh, that their hearts may be encouraged" (Colossians 2:1, ESV)

> The goal is not just our salvation but also that of others. Paul struggled 'for' the church and understood the crucial discipline of prayer. The gospel brings conflict to the entire Christian life, but as we pray and stand together the sign of the cross is a sign of victory.
>
> (Kittel, 21)

The second word for conflict, "athlesis," refers to combat and/or a contest involving athletes who engage in competition or conflict. The word stands behind the English words "athlete" and "athletics." It is used in Hebrews when the author stated, "But recall the former days when, after you were enlightened, you endured a hard struggle with sufferings" (Hebrews 10:32, ESV).

Paul used the word in 2 Timothy 2:5 (ESV) when he wrote to his young, spiritual son and likened all ministries to an athletic contest, wherein the rules must be obeyed. 2 Timothy 2:5 (ESV) suggests the need for exertion, sacrifice, and discipline. In Philippians 1:27 and 4:3 (ESV), συναθλέω (*synathleo*) carries the idea of striving, suffering, and working together. The word "athlesis" in Hebrews 10:32–33 (ESV) evokes the image of public struggle in the arena.

Leadership and conflict go hand in hand. They are inseparable companions. No one who aspires to be a great leader will fail to encounter great conflict. Leadership is uniquely embodied in the person and ministry of a pastor. God-ordained conflict develops qualities of leadership—influence, character, integrity, and discipline—in a way nothing else can. The result is godliness.

Contrary to popular Christian belief, God accomplishes more through conflict in the pastor's life and ministry than success and prosperity ever could. Unfortunately, many in the ministry would rather exchange the refining fire of conflict for the unmistakable dross of ease and comfort. What they fail to realize is that what they have in comfort pales into insignificance when compared to the greater wealth of Christ-likeness acquired through conflict.

This idea is not new. It is as old as the Scriptures. In fact, throughout God's word, men and women became the leaders God wanted them to be by the conflict God brought into their lives. This is a consistent theme.

It is that theme which will be examined in the lives of those found in the biblical text. Both the Old and New Testaments provide numerous examples of people who became godly leaders through the conflicts God permitted to occur. There is valuable information to be found in the Scriptures concerning the indispensability of God-ordained conflict in the development of godly, pastoral leadership. It is to God's inerrant word that our attention is now focused.

CHAPTER TWO

The Theological and Biblical Issues of Conflict: Old Testament Examples

The unfolding drama of God's redemption on behalf of sinful mankind began in Genesis 3. Since the fall, man has been in conflict with God, with the world around him, with Satan, and with his own sin. However, God used conflict and trials as an instrument for His purposes in raising men and women who would faithfully honor and serve Him. The sinner's service to God was often in proportion to the difficulties he or she encountered.

Noah experienced a worldwide devastating flood (Genesis 6–9, ESV). He lived in an ungodly culture where the thoughts of mankind's heart "was only evil continually" (Genesis 6:5, ESV). However, Genesis 6:8 (ESV) explains that Noah remained faithful and "found favor in the eyes of the LORD."

Job probably lived prior to Abraham, Isaac, and Jacob. If anyone encountered conflict, it was he. He lost his possessions, his family (with the notable exception of his wife), his children, and eventually, his health. God permitted this conflict.

In today's culture, the often repeated refrain people pose to God when conflict occurs is, "Why?" From the life lessons in Job, the question posed to God perhaps should be, "Why not!"

Abraham was childless (Genesis 12–21, ESV), but he trusted God's promise that his descendants would be as numerous as the stars in the heavens. Therefore, because of Abraham's faith, God "counted it to him as righteousness" (Genesis 15:6, ESV).

Abraham eventually would have a son, Isaac, but God tested Abraham by asking him to sacrifice his son (Genesis 22:1–2, ESV). Abraham obeyed and would have killed Isaac, but God prevented him when He said, "Do not lay your hand on the boy or do anything to him, for now I know that you fear God, seeing you have not withheld your son, your only son, from me" (Genesis 22:12, ESV) The word "fear" means "reverence" (TWOT, 399). God directed conflict resulted in Abraham trusting and reverencing God.

What was true for Abraham continues to be true for believers today. God permits conflict in our lives, as a means for us to trust Him more and reverence Him greatly.

Jacob, Abraham's grandson, lacked character. He was a liar who manipulated his brother Esau into selling his birthright and deceived his father Isaac by taking Esau's blessing. Jacob was deceitful, but he would learn a valuable lesson when his uncle Laban deceived him. When God changed Jacob's name to Israel, following Jacob's wrestling with God until daybreak, it summarized Jacob's life. Throughout the narratives, Jacob's life had been characterized by struggle, particularly by a struggle to obtain a blessing from God—just as in this narrative. Jacob struggled with his brother, his father, his uncle, and the Lord. However, God used these difficult experiences to ultimately fashion the man who wrestled the Lord for a blessing.

I am sure you have wrestled with God. I know I have. Yet, through those difficulties, God blesses in ways believers could never have imagined.

Joseph, Jacob's son, was a leader. He led his brothers, his family, his fellow prisoners, and eventually, the nation of Egypt. He proved to be a leader regardless of his circumstances. However, his influence was not determined by his situations but rather by his character. Life's conflicts only proved to reveal what was already in his soul.

The struggles God brought into Joseph's life were varied and often unexpected. They included betrayal, abandonment, slavery, false accusations, imprisonment, and disappointment. However, through it all Joseph rested in God's supernatural care.

Do we? I have often found that Christians today tend to elevate biblical characters to a position where they do not belong. We suppose they were more faithful and holy than believers today. Consequently we believe their trials and conflicts pale in comparison to ours. After all, they spoke directly with God, saw His glory, and touched His hand. No wonder they survived. If only we could experience such closeness to God, then our trials and conflicts would not be so dire.

However, the believer in the biblical narrative was no different than the believer today. In fact, believers today are indwelt by the Holy Spirit wherein many Old Testament believers were not. The same God who worked in Joseph's life works in ours.

Joseph's own words testify to his trust in God. Following his father's death, Joseph eased his brother's troubled minds when they suspected he might seek revenge for their unjust treatment of him years earlier. However, Joseph responded by saying, "Do not fear, for am I in the place of God? As for you, you meant evil against me, but God meant it for good, to bring it about that many people should be kept alive, as they are today" (Genesis

50:19–20, ESV). Joseph knew firsthand that "God causes all things to work together for good" (Romans 8.28, NASB).

Eventually, Jacob's family of seventy, over the course of 430 years (Exodus 12:41, ESV) would multiply to over six hundred thousand men (Exodus 12:37, ESV; Numbers 1:46, ESV), allowing for a total population of close to two million. God had kept His promise to Abraham (Genesis 12:1–3, ESV; 15:1–6, ESV; 22:15–18, ESV), Isaac (Genesis 26:23–25, ESV), and Jacob (Genesis 28:13–15, ESV; 35:9–11, ESV). Israel's family was now a nation; unfortunately, they became a nation in bondage to Egypt.

God uses individuals in times of conflict who are uniquely prepared by Him. This is in order to meet the challenges of a particular moment. Moses was just such an individual. You may be also. Throughout his life in the Egyptian court, in the backside of a desert, and eventually, leading Israel to the Promised Land, Moses encountered enough conflict for three lifetimes. However, he remained a man of faith and grew into a man of God.

Moses would encounter conflict time and again through Israel's journey back home. The people complained about hunger, they erected a golden calf for idolatrous worship, they complained about the food, and even Moses' brother and sister, Aaron and Miriam, criticized him with devastating results.

In addition, the nation failed to trust God at Kadesh-Barnea resulting in their refusal to enter Canaan. God was ready to destroy them, but Moses interceded on their behalf, imploring God to spare them while acknowledging that "the LORD is slow to anger and abounding in steadfast love, forgiving iniquity and transgression, but he will by no means clear the guilty, visiting the iniquity of the fathers on the children, to the third and the fourth generation" (Numbers 14:18, ESV). The Lord pardoned, in part, because of Moses' words, but He would only allow the younger generation to enter Canaan, while their parents would die in the wilderness. Further conflict ensued when Israel suddenly changed its mind and attempted to enter Canaan only to encounter defeat when a Sabbath-breaker was stoned and when Korah rebelled against Moses's leadership resulting in the 250 people involved in the conspiracy being swallowed up by the ground.

Through all these conflicts, along with many others, Moses remained faithful and true to God. However, there was one exception: his failure to trust God at the waters of Meribah. The consequence was that God denied Moses entrance into the land he had anticipated entering for forty years. Moses learned that even leaders can be disciplined when they fail to hallow God before a congregation (Numbers 20:7–12, ESV).

The scandals that astounded and shocked the supporters of televangelists Jim Bakker and Jimmy Swaggert a generation ago reminded us that once a leader loses his credibility, he loses his influence. While both these men remain in some facet of ministry, whether or not they should be, one thing remains clear: they do not have the influential leadership platform they once had. They were entrusted with a sacred stewardship and they violated that trust. However, rather than judge these two, and others, too harshly, let us always remember that "let anyone who thinks that he stands take heed lest he fall" (1 Corinthians 10:12, ESV).

As the nation of Israel was poised at the Jordan River to enter Canaan, God raised a new leader: Joshua. The book of Joshua covers a period of about twenty-five years. The book describes the invasion, conquest, and settlement of Palestine by the nation, Israel. God used conflict throughout this period of conquest to develop Joshua's leadership ability and strengthen Israel.

Following a period of purification and preparation, Israel began to conquer the land God gave them. A victory at Jericho, however, was immediately followed by a crushing defeat at Ai. Joshua's reaction was significant. He questioned God as to why

He allowed this defeat to occur. Joshua said, "Alas, O Lord GOD, why have you brought this people over the Jordan at all, to give us into the hands of the Amorites, to destroy us? Would that we had been content to dwell beyond the Jordan!" (Joshua 7:7, ESV).

When conflict occurs, leaders may blame God for their circumstances. They cannot understand why God would allow such a thing to occur. However, a closer look at the situation often reveals that rather than God being unjust, the leader, or his group, may have sinned.

When former United States President Bill Clinton was being assailed for his alleged impropriety with a White House intern, his supporters rallied behind him asserting how unfair the political opposition was being. A vast right-wing conspiracy was targeted as the real villain in the situation. Get rid of them, and you will get rid of the problems plaguing the president.

However, it soon became evident that the president indeed had "sex with that woman" and the subsequent impeachment procedures were directly caused by his sin and his efforts to cover it up. Even though his supporters remained steadfastly behind him, the president did eventually apologize for his indiscretion. His public act of contrition was in direct contrast to those who endeavored to demonize his critics. However, for many his presidential legacy would forever be tainted.

This is what occurred at Ai. Israel's victory at Jericho would always be spoiled because of Achan taking the accursed things from the city. This act resulted in God's judgment upon Israel at Ai. The only way God would bless Israel was if they dealt with the sin.

Achan eventually confessed his sin resulting in he, and his entire family, being stoned to death and burned with fire. The seriousness of this scene is second only to the seriousness of the sin that precipitated it. Joshua learned that God permits conflict in order to chastise and cleanse His people from their sinful choices. A wise pastor or leader will first look at his own heart relationship with God, and that of his congregation's or company, before blaming God for injustice.

Joshua's final address to the people reminded them of God's goodness. He warned them concerning disobedience and challenged them to serve God with all their heart. However, the lessons Israel learned when they conquered Palestine would often be forgotten as they settled the Promised Land.

The period of the Judges was "the saddest and most sordid period in the entire history of Israel. It is the dark ages of that nation" (Wilmington, 91). The recorded time involved some three hundred years and included such important characters as Ruth, Gideon, Samson, Naomi, Boaz, Eli, and Samuel.

There were seven cycles of apostasy committed by Israel during these three centuries. These apostasies were followed respectively by seven bondages to ungodly nations and, eventually, seven deliverances by God. "The following two outlines have been suggested to summarize the Judges Stage: rebellion, retribution, repentance, and restoration, or sin, servitude, supplication and salvation" (Wilmington 91).

The absence of a godly leader to replace Joshua was a key issue. The book of Judges records the following evaluation of Israel's walk with God: "In those days there was no king in Israel. Everyone did what was right in his own eyes" (Judges 21:25, ESV). Israel compromised in disobeying God by failing to drive out her enemies. The nation also apostatized by doing what God forbade which was worshiping idols: the gods of her enemies.

However, God continued to love Israel, and He raised fifteen judges to serve, not so much as legal experts, but as military deliverers. In addition, the Angel of the Lord is mentioned over twenty times in Judges. "It is thought by most theologians that the Angel of the Lord in the Old Testament was none other than Christ himself. Therefore, during no other stage does God so minister to His people" (Wilmington 91).

It should be noted that the judges God provided Israel were flawed individuals. They made rash vows, were doubtful, and were lustful. However, God used what He had in order to minister during a time of great defeat, slavery, unbelief, weakness, sorrow, and strife. During conflict, God may choose to use the most available, rather than the most spiritual. He may choose to use individuals such as a Jephthah, a Gideon, or a Samson to accomplish his work. These were tremendously flawed people whom God used in spite of their failures.

However, the period of the Judges would culminate with Samuel. He was not only a godly man, but he would also become the transitional figure God used when He ceased raising up judges and began to establish a kingdom though the united monarchy of Saul, David, and Solomon.

The united kingdom stage involves the books of I Samuel 8–31(ESV), 2 Samuel (ESV), I Kings 1–11(ESV), 1 Chronicles (ESV), 2 Chronicles 1–9 (ESV), Psalms (ESV), Proverbs (ESV), Ecclesiastes (ESV), and Song of Solomon (ESV). It covers a period of 120 years with Saul, David, and Solomon ruling respectively for forty years. The period begins with the choice of a king to rule the united land (Saul) and concludes with the rejection of another king (Rehoboam) as the land becomes divided.

Valuable lessons can be learned, even from a superficial examination of Saul, David, and Solomon, regarding the kind of leaders God desires and develops. Leaders can glean much from these historical narratives in what they should, and should not, do when God calls them into ministry.

With respect to King Saul, today's leader must avoid the mistake of making rash decisions and holding to a philosophy of pragmatism in which the ends justify the means. God rejected Saul because he offered a priestly sacrifice when it clearly was disobedient to God's law to do so. Saul also inadvertently ordered the death of his own son, Jonathan, and disobeyed God's command to completely destroy Agag and his city of Amalek as God instructed. This prompted God to tell Samuel, "I regret that I have made Saul king, for he has turned back from following me and has not performed my commandments." And Samuel was angry, and he cried to the Lord all night" (1 Samuel 15:11, ESV). Following Saul's lame excuse in justifying his behavior, Samuel rebuked the king. He said:

> Has the Lord *as great delight* in burnt offerings and sacrifices, as in obeying the voice of the Lord? Behold, to obey is better than sacrifice, and to heed the fat of rams. For rebellion is as the sin of witchcraft, and stubbornness is as iniquity and idolatry. Because you have rejected the word of the Lord, He also has rejected you from being king.
>
> (1 Samuel 15:22–23, ESV)

In addition, Saul became possessed by an evil spirit, attempted to kill David, cursed and deliberately attempted to kill Jonathan his son, slaughtered eighty-five of God's priests, along with visiting a witch. Saul became a leader on the downgrade.

When conflict occurs, the godly leader must never do what he believes is right when those beliefs contradict God's word. If he does violate God's standard, he finds himself in the precarious position of losing God's blessing. A leader's stubborn convictions may result in him selfishly serving his own desires rather than obeying God. When conflict comes, the resolution of the conflict never justifies the usage of any means necessary. This is what happened to King Saul.

Following graduation from college, I began working in a Christian high school as a Bible and social studies teacher. The school was affiliated with, and under the auspices of, a local church of which I did not attend. Soon after I left the school to accept another ministerial position elsewhere, the church was investigated by the United States Internal Revenue Service for failure to pay Social Security taxes on behalf of its school teachers, even when those monies had been previously withheld from their pay. This violation of financial integrity was due to the church's increasing indebtedness and the leadership's decision to use whatever means necessary to meet those financial obligations.

The situation became public. The surrounding communities became aware of this significant scandal. The character of the gospel of Jesus Christ was impugned due to a church's actions in the face of rising conflict and the decision to use whatever means necessary to resolve the conflict. While the church continues to function, its reputation was forever soiled.

King Saul never recovered from his personal implosion. God's rejection of Saul resulted in the Lord seeking a new king: a man after His own heart. God instructed Samuel, "Do not look on his appearance or on the height of his stature, because I have rejected him. For the Lord sees not as man sees: man looks on the outward appearance, but the Lord looks on the heart" (1 Samuel 16:7, esv). David would be this man after God's own heart.

David was a shepherd, a singer, and a soldier. King Saul would seek to kill David because of his jealousy over David's popularity and anointment as king. Following Saul's death, David would become the sovereign king of Israel.

David's life can be chronicled by his rise to power, which was followed by his fall from greatness. His descent, and the conflict his family encountered, can be traced back not only to his sin with Bathsheba but also when he took many wives and concubines.

> We must note, and note well, that David's taking additional wives was sin. Deuteronomy 17, which set down the standards for Hebrew kings, commanded that they refrain from three things: acquiring many horses, taking many wives, and accumulating much silver and gold. David did fine on one and three, but he completely failed on number two by willfully collecting a considerable harem. (Hughes, 23)

Godly leaders must never permit themselves to become desensitized to the dangers of sexual temptation. David did and with that came relaxation, fixation, rationalization, and eventually, degeneration into adultery, lies, and murder.

On his deathbed, David exhorted his son Solomon to do the following when he became king: to act like a man of God, to be true to the Word of God, to rely on the promises of God, and to execute the judgment of God. These are disciplines worthy of a leader's notice anytime but certainly during conflict. David, unfortunately, was inconsistent in these disciplines. Therefore, his legacy was tainted and inconsistent.

What legacy did Solomon leave? Solomon was Israel's most successful king. He triumphed over his enemies, he requested, and received, wisdom from God, and the tranquility existing in Israel at this time foreshadowed the millennial reign of Christ. The crowning achievement of Solomon's reign was the construction of the temple. Solomon's reputation became universally known.

However, Solomon sinned against God in three areas: he had much silver and gold, he owned thousands of horses, and he gathered hundreds of wives and concubines. As his father before him, Solomon violated the commandments of Deuteronomy 17:14–17 (ESV).

If God does not bring conflict and trials into a leader's life in order to refine him, he may bring difficulties in order to punish him. God plagued Solomon with troublemakers and minor revolts for the rest of his life because "the LORD was angry with Solomon, because his heart had turned away from the LORD, the God of Israel, who had appeared to him twice" (1 Kings 11:9, ESV). As further punishment after his death, God would give a large portion of Solomon's kingdom to his servant and only one tribe to his son Rehoboam. The united kingdom became divided, chaotic, and sinful.

What legacy are you preparing to leave? Mind you, I am not speaking about finances or property. Rather, I am referring to leaving the lasting heritage of godliness, character, and integrity. This is beyond measure and is the refined result of God's benevolent mercy in bringing conflict into the leader's life. I am striving to leave my children, and grandchildren, the legacy of a godly father and grandfather who became refined in the character of Christ by the crucible of conflicts.

The divided kingdom period lasted for approximately 325 years from 931 BC to 605 BC. The major events took place in Samaria and Jerusalem and are recounted in the historical books of 1 Kings 12–22 (ESV), 2 Kings 1–17 (ESV), 2 Chronicles 10–36 (ESV), and the prophetical books of Jonah, Amos, Hosea, Joel, Obadiah, Nahum, Isaiah, Micah, Habakkuk, Zephaniah, Jeremiah, and Lamentations.

Israel split after Solomon's death, and a tragic civil war ensued. Ten tribes established the northern kingdom of Israel, while two tribes, Judah and Benjamin, established the southern kingdom of Judah. What began violently concluded the same way with

Israel's enslavement to Assyria in 722 Bc and Judah's defeat by Babylon in 605 Bc.

During this time of miracles, battles, and many prophecies from God, there were nineteen kings in the north and twenty in the south. All of the northern kings were evil, and many were assassinated, killed in battle, or committed suicide. However, in the southern kingdom, there were eight righteous rulers who served the Lord by doing what was right. It was not always easy, and they were not perfect men, but the majority of these eight rulers faithfully followed the Lord in times of intense conflict. These kings were Asa, Jehoshaphat, Joash, Amaziah, Uzziah, Jotham, Hezekiah, and Josiah.

During this time, there were also oral and writing prophets. They also encountered conflict, and they too were not perfect men. Three of them are highlighted below.

Elijah fled from Queen Jezebel and asked God to kill him when she announced her intentions to kill the prophet within twenty-four hours following the defeat of the prophets of Baal at Mount Carmel. However, Elijah learned that even though he was fearful, he could turn to God in whose grace there would be sufficiency.

God ordered him to start preaching again, telling him that he was not alone as he thought, to anoint a new king for Syria, to anoint Jehu to be king of Israel, and to begin training a successor. Elijah's ministry came to an end when God took him into heaven in a whirlwind (2 Kings 2:1–11, ESV).

The Prophet Jonah did not flee from an evil queen but rather from God instead of preaching repentance to the city of Nineveh (Jonah 1, ESV). God wanted Nineveh saved, but Jonah wanted it destroyed. God used extreme circumstances, a storm and a great fish, to bring Jonah to a place of preparedness for ministry.

However, even though Jonah preached and the people of Nineveh repented and believed, the prophet was despondent and angry at God and wanted to die. He did not want the Ninevites spared from God's judgment. Ironically, his greater pity was for a dying plant rather than dying people.

God told the prophet it was well within His prerogative to have pity on His creation as Jonah had pity on a plant: a form of life in which he contributed nothing to its creation or growth. Throughout these conflicts, God raised Jonah to become more than what he had been. This was also the case with Jeremiah.

Jeremiah was the son of the priest Hilkiah. At first, Jeremiah protested God's call for him to be a prophet, arguing that he could not speak and that he was too young. However, God informed him that He had chosen him to serve before he was born. "Now the word of the Lord came to me, saying, 'Before I formed you in the womb I knew you, and before you were born I consecrated you; I appointed you a prophet to the nations" (Jeremiah 1:4–5, ESV).

Furthermore, the Lord said, "Do not say, 'I am only a youth'; for to all to whom I send you, you shall go, and whatever I command you, you shall speak. Do not be afraid of them, for I am with you to deliver you, declares the Lord" (Jeremiah 1:7–8, ESV). In addition, God said, "Behold, I have put my words in your mouth. See, I have set you this day over nations and over kingdoms, to pluck up and to break down, to destroy and to overthrow, to build and to plant" (Jeremiah 1:9–10, ESV).

Jeremiah's ministry was steeped in conflict. He pleaded with Judah to return to God and fearlessly denounced the nation's sin. In return, his family, the people of his hometown of Anathoth, and the priests and other religious leaders persecuted him.

However, Jeremiah remained faithful and continued to warn Judah about the upcoming Babylonian captivity. He proclaimed that Jerusalem would be surrounded by her enemies, that her own trees would be used against her, that the temple would be destroyed, the corpses of Jews would feed animals, and the ensuing captivity would last seventy years.

Jeremiah wept over this impending judgment and at one point even threatened to resign because the lack of receptivity by the nation of Judah to his preaching. He also cursed the day of his birth. He soon realized that God's word was in his heart. "If I say, 'I will not mention him, or speak any more in his name,' there is in my heart as it were a burning fire shut up in my bones, and I am weary with holding it in, and I cannot" (Jeremiah 20:9, ESV).

He knew people were mocking him and even plotting to kill him, yet he possessed a strong assurance God was with him. "But the LORD is with me as a dread warrior; therefore my persecutors will stumble; they will not overcome me. They will be greatly shamed, for they will not succeed. Their eternal dishonor will never be forgotten" (Jeremiah 20:11, ESV).

Jeremiah also realized that it was through this tremendous time of conflict that God tested and tried him. "O LORD of hosts, who tests the righteous, who sees the heart and the mind, let me see your vengeance upon them, for to you have I committed my cause" (Jeremiah 20:12, ESV).

Jeremiah served as a prophet under Judah's final four kings, as well as the Babylonian conqueror, Nebuchadnezzar; the Babylonian governor, Gedaliah; and Johanan, Gedaliah's successor. The circumstances of his life were difficult and often dangerous. However, he remained a dedicated servant of God. He wanted, and would have enjoyed, a wife, children, friends, and the respect of his fellow countrymen. All these were denied to him.

What he possessed instead was an extremely intimate relationship with God, fired and refined by the circumstances he faced as a prophet of God. It is for the latter, and not the former, that he is remembered. In our walk with God, what is it that people will remember about us?

God's presence and provision also benefited those who followed Jeremiah in ministering to Judah during its seventy-year exile in Babylon. One such individual who grew as a leader during conflict was Daniel.

> Tests of character are the toughest tests to pass. Tougher than state bar exams, medical boards, and orals for a Ph.D. all rolled into one. Why? Because when our integrity is on the line, we must go beyond mere knowledge and dig deep to the very bedrock of who we are. Character tests expose our hidden flaws; but they also reveal our strengths—our determination to love, our commitment to honesty, our faith in God.
>
> (Swindoll 10)

In October 1999, I had the privilege of attending a leadership conference at Dallas Theological Seminary. During a four-day period, I sat under the teaching ministry of such leaders as Chuck Swindoll, Joseph Stowell, and Howard Hendricks. I returned home filled to overflowing.

The conference's theme was "Into the Eye of the Storm: Serving with Courage in Turbulent Times." I did not realize then that the information these men taught during that week would prepare me for my own "eye of the storm" several years later.

Dr. Hendricks entitled his plenary sessions *Cameos of Character*. He led us through a biblical study of character. He cited several authors regarding the issue of leadership and character, but one quote resonated with me. It was A. W. Tozer who wrote,

"God never uses anyone greatly until He tests them deeply." One such man whom God tested deeply was Daniel.

In the Old Testament book of Daniel, God portrays Daniel's life in panorama, not only as a teenager in chapter one but also as an elderly man in chapter six. Despite the passing of close to seventy years, Daniel remained a man of character in the midst of conflict while he served in captivity through three administrations. He stood tall under God's guidance.

The opening verses of Daniel provide the immediate historical context:

> In the third year of the reign of Jehoiakim king of Judah, Nebuchadnezzar king of Babylon came to Jerusalem and besieged it. And the Lord gave Jehoiakim king of Judah into his hand, with some of the vessels of the house of God. And he brought them to the land of Shinar, to the house of his god, and placed the vessels in the treasury of his god.
>
> (Daniel 1:1–2, ESV)

Babylon had besieged Judah. Having defeated the Egyptians at Carchemish in 605 BC, King Nebuchadnezzar enjoyed victories in Syria and Palestine, swallowing up smaller nations like Judah. The attack on Jerusalem resulted in Judean King Jehoiakim's quick surrender and an agreement that Judah would be a slave state. 2 Kings 24:8–25:21(ESV) and Lamentations 4 (ESV) chronicles these historical events. Additionally, Nebuchadnezzar instructed his master of eunuchs, Ashpenaz, to select some of the best and the brightest of Judah's young men, including Jehoiakim's descendants and some of the nobles, to be taken to Babylon where they would serve the king (Daniel 1:3–4, ESV).

The term "young men" in Hebrew is יֶלֶד (*ben*) (TWOT, 113–114). This suggests that they may not have been older than seventeen and no younger than thirteen or fourteen. These young men had to be physically free from any handicaps or bodily blemish; they had to be good-looking, wise, intelligent, understanding, and socially poised. They would be taught the language and literature of the Chaldeans and undergo three years of intensive training so "at the end of that time they were to stand before the king" (Daniel 1:5, ESV).

These individuals had to look good, possess the ability to make decisions, be good students, be quick to understand facts and come to conclusions, and have the proper manners and social graces not to embarrass the king in the palace. It is obvious that King Nebuchadnezzar desired only a few good men.

The young captives' names were even changed in order to indoctrinate them into the culture of the Babylonians. "Among these were Daniel, Hananiah, Mishael, and Azariah of the tribe of Judah. And the chief of the eunuchs gave them names: Daniel he called Belteshazzar, Hananiah he called Shadrach, Mishael he called Meshach, and Azariah he called Abednego" (Daniel 1:6–7, ESV). "Obviously, pagan theocratic names like these must have been assigned arbitrarily to these four Israelite students without any consultation with them, since the new names contained the names of false gods" (Archer, 34). As Dr. Leon Wood writes:

> There were reasons for making such changes, however, and here it was certainly to make the young men more Babylonian. If they were eventually to make good governmental personnel, they should become more Babylonian in their thinking and manner of life as soon as possible; and Babylonian-type names should help. (Wood, 36)

The Scriptures continue to say that "the king assigned them a daily portion of the food that the king ate, and of the wine that he drank" (Daniel 1:5, ESV). It is at this point that Daniel and his friends made a decision. "But Daniel resolved that he would not defile himself with the king's food, or with the wine that he drank. Therefore he asked the chief of the eunuchs to allow him not to defile himself" (Daniel 1:8, ESV).

Daniel and his three friends were asked to do four things: receive a pagan education, serve in a prominent position, submit to a name change to reflect pagan deities, and eat and drink the king's food. However, all of them refused only one of the requests: to eat the king's food. Why?

Please notice that the first three requests were beyond the young men's ability to refuse. They were prisoners of Babylon, but given the opportunity to advance into positions of prominence and influence. The first three stipulations would not necessarily cause them to compromise their integrity of character because a secular education was not necessarily evil, if one discerns truth from error by adhering to a divine standard.

However, eating the king's food was another matter. The reasons for the defilement, which they saw, would have been basically twofold: first, Jewish dietary laws prohibited the eating of certain types of food (Leviticus 11, ESV), and second, the meat would have been offered to the Babylonian gods. As to the first, to eat the food would have been to disobey God's direct command in the Law; and as to the second, it would give recognition, though in an indirect manner, to the existence of Babylonian gods. Daniel was convinced that eating the food would mean defiling themselves. They refused to do so. Daniel and his friends committed to not compromise.

When facing conflict, people often take the path of least resistance. They compromise and accommodate rather than confront the conflict by maintaining a righteous conviction and refusing to participate in ungodly behavior. Daniel and his friends could have compromised. They had every reason to do so. They were far from home, the pressure was great, and they were disobeying authority and probably risking execution. Yet they would not give in to the king's demands.

It would have been natural to argue that since God had not protected them from this captivity, they did not have to be careful in obeying His demands. Too many Christians do this in comparable situations, rationalizing that if God has not been "fair" with them, they do not have to be good Christians themselves. The young men could have become bitter because of having been taken from home, but if they had, they never would have been able to make the fine decision they did.

> And God gave Daniel favor and compassion in the sight of the chief of the eunuchs, and the chief of the eunuchs said to Daniel, "I fear my lord the king, who assigned your food and your drink; for why should he see that you were in worse condition than the youths who are of your own age? So you would endanger my head with the king. (Daniel 1:9–10, ESV)

Ashpenaz was worried, not for Daniel and his friends but for himself. He was concerned that if the four lads looked worse than the other young men their age, he was going to be killed. Notice that Ashpenaz referred to other young men Daniel's age who were under, supposedly, the same directives. However, they went along with the king's edicts. They apparently compromised, even though they possibly were from the same heritage as Daniel.

Conflict reveals an individual's character or the lack thereof. Trials illuminate what an individual truly is rather than what a man would like people to believe he is. This is what distinguishes a man as a leader rather than a pretender.

In the classic television series *The Fugitive*, the main character, Dr. Richard Kimble, is accused, tried, convicted, and sentenced to the death penalty for his wife's murder. However, he is innocent. Freed from his police escort, Lieutenant Gerard, because the train taking him to prison derails, Richard Kimble becomes a fugitive while at the same time attempting to locate the "one-armed man" he believes is responsible for his wife's death.

Following a four-year quest from imprisonment and for justice, Richard Kimble finally confronts the "one-armed man" and extracts a confession. Unfortunately, the criminal dies with having only confessed to Dr. Kimble. He returns to the custody of Lieutenant Gerard, and they both realize the fate awaiting this fugitive.

Ironically, a neighbor of the Kimble's comes to his eventual reclamation. He witnessed the "one-armed man" commit the murder. He was in the Kimble's home the night of the murder and saw everything. He finally agrees to testify.

Why did he not come forward at the initial trial and testify to what he had seen? It was because he cowered in fear, even while Helen Kimble screamed for his help as she fought with the "one-armed man" who came to rob the family. The neighbor prided himself as a hunter, a war hero, and one in whom the entire neighborhood could count on whenever trouble occurred. Yet at this crucial moment, he feared for his own life rather than save the life of another. Afterward to protect his image, instead of revealing the real killer's identity and the reality of his cowardice, he was willing to let Richard Kimble be executed for a crime he did not commit.

Unlike this fictional character, Daniel's integrity shone brightly! Faced with a difficult situation, he did not cower in fear. Rather, Daniel pursued a reasonable alternative:

> Then Daniel said to the steward whom the chief of the eunuchs had assigned over Daniel, Hananiah, Mishael, and Azariah, "Test your servants for ten days; let us be given vegetables to eat and water to drink. Then let our appearance and the appearance of the youths who eat the king's food be observed by you, and deal with your servants according to what you see." So he listened to them in this matter, and tested them for ten days.
>
> (Daniel 1:11–14, ESV)

What was the result of Daniel's diplomatic suggestion? At the end of ten days, Daniel and his three friends looked better and healthier than everyone else who indulged the king's food. Therefore, "the steward took away their food and the wine they were to drink, and gave them vegetables" (Daniel 1:16, ESV).

When King Nebuchadnezzar interviewed all the young men in his service, he found no one to match the abilities of Daniel, Hananiah, Mishael, and Azariah. In fact, "in every matter of wisdom and understanding about which the king inquired of them, he found them ten times better than all the magicians and enchanters that were in all his kingdom" (Daniel 1:20, ESV).

Why was Daniel so confident that things would turn out right? Perhaps it is because Daniel recognized that when God is all you have, God is all you need. "When a person is living a holy life, he has a sense of invincibility that believes God will deliver. Daniel had that kind of unblemished faith" (MacArthur, 57). Daniel's faith stood the test of time. He never wavered in his uncompromising commitment to God, either as a young man or when he was older.

In Daniel 6, the young teenager we met in chapter one is an elderly man nearing ninety. He had witnessed Babylon's fall along with the rise of Medo-Persia. Throughout his life, Daniel received many blessings from God. What Daniel gave back to God was an unwavering commitment to godliness.

As the chapter unfolds, Cyrus, also known as King Darius, is in power. "It pleased Darius to set over the kingdom 120 satraps, to be throughout the whole kingdom" (Daniel 6:1, ESV). A satrap was an administrator who served the king. Over these satraps were three governors who kept the 120 administrators accountable for the king's revenue. "The reason for the appointment of the governors appears to have been a royal concern over deceit and graft" (Ferguson, 128). Daniel was one of these three governors.

As governor, Daniel distinguished himself admirably. In fact, "Daniel became distinguished above all the other high officials and satraps, because an excellent spirit was in him" (Daniel 6:3, ESV).

The phrase "excellent spirit" means "preeminent or surpassing" (TWOT, 1030). Daniel surpassed the other governors so completely that "the king planned to set him over the whole kingdom" (Daniel 6:3b, ESV).

One sure way a leader encounters conflict is when people become jealous of the leader's success. They not only want what the leader has, but they also resent the leader having what he has. This obsession can lead to all sorts of opposition, even in a church. How unfortunate when an associate pastor, envying the respect and success of a senior pastor, vies for that respect and success by undermining the pastor. Hoping to acquire the pastor's position and popularity, the associate subtly attacks the pastor's credibility and character. Eventually, lines are drawn, sides are taken, and a church splits.

The associate pastor has achieved his goal and begins his own church, but at what a cost? Lives and reputations have been damaged. People have been hurt. The credibility of the gospel has been questioned because of the behavior of believers.

However, "the soundness, the integrity of our faith and character is what will keep us standing in the midst of life's storms—just as they did for Daniel" (Swindoll, 62). Daniel's storm of conflict hit hard and fast, much like a tropical depression that becomes a category five hurricane in a matter of hours resulting in a furious, meteorological monster devastating everything in its path. What happened to Daniel?

The other governors, and all of the satraps, conspired against Daniel. They "sought to find a ground for complaint against Daniel with regard to the kingdom, but they could find no ground for complaint or any fault, because he was faithful, and no error or fault was found in him" (Daniel 6:4, ESV). Because of their intense jealousy of Daniel, his enemies sought to bring charges against him. However, they could find no charge or fault. Why? The reason no fault could be found in Daniel was because he was faithful to God. He had an excellent attitude, he was faithful in his work, and he maintained purity in his relationships.

This would not deter Daniel's enemies. They sought all the more to find some allegation to use against him. They reasoned that the only way to accuse him of wrongdoing before the king would be in relation to Daniel's faith in God (Daniel 6:5, ESV). "Criticisms can break us or create us. That which does not break us makes us stronger. Good timber does not grow with ease; the stronger the wind, the stronger the trees" (Miller, 36). When people cannot accuse you of wrongdoing, they will find what is good in your life and make it appear inappropriate.

When I was a youth pastor, I encountered an increasing lack of trust within the church where I was serving. Not only was there a lack of trust by the congregation toward the church board, but there was also the same lack of confidence among the board members toward the pastoral staff. It made for a very difficult atmosphere.

On one occasion, the church board requested that each pastor submit an accounting of his weekly hours. This was meant to give the church board an understanding and insight into the amount of hours each pastor worked, not including emergencies and unexpected situations. When the hours were submitted, members of the board criticized the pastoral staff about the amount of hours indicated. Some disbelieved any pastor would work more than forty hours per week. Some even "subtly" accused the pastoral staff of lying, or padding their hours, to appear more spiritual. The lack of trust arose again with the church board finding fault with the pastors' work ethic. This situation, instead of being a blessing, became a source of grief for the pastoral staff, not only by the church board but also by the congregation. This is what Daniel encountered.

"Then these high officials and satraps came by agreement to the king" (Daniel 6:6, ESV). Came by agreement means "to gather tumultuously" (Strong, 106) or "to be in tumult" (TWOT, 1071). A tumult is "a disorderly crowd" or "an angry demonstration by a mob" (Oxford, 892). The king's advisors were so incensed at Daniel that they were like a mob causing a riot. They quickly devised their plan.

> O King Darius, live forever! All the high officials of the kingdom, the prefects and the satraps, the counselors and the governors are agreed that the king should establish an ordinance and enforce an injunction, that whoever makes petition to any god or man for thirty days, except to you, O king, shall be cast into the den of lions. Now, O king, establish the injunction and sign the document, so that it cannot be changed, according to the law of the Medes and the Persians, which cannot be revoked." Therefore King Darius signed the document and injunction. (Daniel 6:6–9, ESV)

The governors came to the king and lied. How? By saying "all of the governors of the kingdom" had consulted together to establish the decree. There were only three governors and Daniel was one of them and they certainly had not consulted him. Creators of conflict will say and do anything to accomplish their intended goal of opposing and destroying the individual of whom they are jealous. There is nothing they will not try and no depths they will not stoop to accomplish their task. This makes for a frightening situation, not only for Daniel but also for modern-day leaders. It is one thing when the attacks come from unbelievers, but it is especially hurtful when the jealous attackers profess to be Christians.

Did Darius realize his governors played him for a fool? He most likely did not; at least, not at first. However, notice what Daniel did. The Scriptures make it abundantly clear that Daniel did not give a moment's hesitation regarding what he should do. "When Daniel knew that the document had been signed, he went to his house where he had windows in his upper chamber open toward Jerusalem. He got down on his knees three times a day and prayed and gave thanks before his God, as he had done previously" (Daniel 6:10, ESV).

Daniel went home, and with his windows open, he knelt down, and he prayed three times that day. Also notice that this was a pattern of behavior he had done since he had been a youth. Daniel's uncompromising commitment to God never wavered throughout his life. It did not matter who was in charge of the government or what difficulties he encountered. He maintained a vibrant prayer life, regardless of the consequences, which in this case would mean certain death by being cast into a den of lions.

It did not take long for the governors and the satraps to take advantage of the situation. They assembled and went before the king saying:

> O king! Did you not sign an injunction, that anyone who makes petition to any god or man within thirty days except to you, O king, shall be cast into the den of lions? The king answered and said, The thing stands fast, according to the law of the Medes and Persians, which cannot be revoked. (Daniel 6:12, ESV)

Darius responded that "the thing is true, according to the law of the Medes and Persians, which does not alter" (Daniel 6:12, ESV). Notice that the law could not be changed for the specified period of time. It was then the conspirators went in for the kill. "Then they answered and said before the king, 'Daniel, who is one of the exiles from Judah, pays no attention to you, O king, or the injunction you have signed, but makes his petition three times a day'"(Daniel 6:13, ESV).

The sense of disdain they had for Daniel is evident when they called him "that Daniel." They further identified him as "one of the captives from Judah" perhaps indicating their Persian nationality and subsequent prejudice.

There is a common practice among politicians called spin doctoring. A spin doctor is a political pundit employed to promote a favorable interpretation of developments to the media. It is making what is wrong appear to be right and to deflect any criticism from themselves by directing it toward someone else. The governors and satraps obviously knew this tactic for they deflected their evil intentions and ill regard for the king by seeking to convince the king it was Daniel who did not respect him. However, by this time, King Darius realized he had been duped by the very governors and satraps he had naively trusted. "Then the king, when he heard these words, was much distressed and set his mind to deliver Daniel. And he labored till the sun went down to rescue him" (Daniel 6:14, ESV).

Darius knew the kind of man Daniel was and by now realized the type of men the governors and satraps were. He made every effort to rescind the law, and its verdict, until the day was over. Alas, it was to no avail because Persian law dictated a decree could not be changed. The governors and satraps eagerly sought to remind the king of this important fact. They said, "Know, O king, that it is a law of the Medes and Persians that no injunction or ordinance that the king establishes can be changed" (Daniel 6:15, ESV). Darius had no choice.

So the king gave the command, and they brought Daniel and cast him into the den of lions (Daniel 6.16, ESV). Who cast Daniel into the den of lions? The text says "they." Who were "they?" Probably the governors and the satraps for this would be their crowning moment of victory. It would be most fitting for them to be the ones who actually threw Daniel into this den of certain death. It would be their complete triumph over one they despised so completely. Creators of conflict will stop at nothing until they have achieved their goal.

Even though Darius believed that Daniel's doom was certain, he still spoke to Daniel and said, "May your God, whom you serve continually, deliver you" (Daniel 6:16, ESV). Notice that Darius knew Daniel's character and his personal integrity. He knew Daniel served God faithfully. He also knew that God would protect Daniel even though the text does not indicate that Darius knew Daniel's God.

Then, much like a climactic scene to a season ending episode of a television series, " a stone was brought and laid on the mouth of the den, and the king sealed it with his own signet and with the signet of his lords, that nothing might be changed concerning Daniel" (Daniel 6:17, ESV). Would Daniel survive? Would the governors and the satraps accomplish their dastardly plan? Would the man who stood for godly integrity become the victim of those who represented ungodly pragmatism and hypocrisy? It almost seems that the next words appearing in the text should be "to be continued."

Darius did not sleep that night. He could not. A trusted advisor faced certain death, and Darius was ultimately responsible. The text says that Darius "went to his palace and spent the night fasting; no diversions were brought to him, and sleep fled from him" (Daniel 6:18, ESV). It must have been the longest night of his life. So it is when creators of conflict appear to have won. All seems hopeless.

Darius got up very early the next morning. The text says that "at break of day, the king arose and went in haste to the den of lions" (Daniel 6:19, ESV). What did Darius do when he arrived at the den? He cried out with a loud voice saying, "O Daniel, servant of the living God, has your God, whom you serve continually, been able to deliver you from the lions" (Daniel 6:20, ESV)? Darius did not call Daniel his servant but rather God's servant. The king knew to whom Daniel ultimately was responsible. He also knew that only Daniel's God could save him.

Then what must have been a most joyful sound came to Darius' ears. It was Daniel's voice saying, "O king, live forever! My God sent his angel and shut the lions' mouths, and they have not harmed me, because I was found blameless before him; and also before you, O king, I have done no harm" (Daniel 6:21–22, ESV).

Darius was overjoyed. The text says he "was exceedingly glad" (Daniel 6.23, ESV). The king commanded that Daniel be removed from the lion's den. Daniel was uninjured. There was no mark on him. No scratches or anything. Why? The text says it was because Daniel believed in his God (Daniel 6:23, ESV).

As Daniel gave praise to God, and so did Darius. However, it did not come in the fashion one might imagine. Scripture says

"And the king commanded, and those men who had maliciously accused Daniel were brought and cast into the den of lions—they, their children, and their wives. And before they reached the bottom of the den, the lions overpowered them and broke all their bones in pieces" (Daniel 6:24, ESV). Conflict has consequences not only for its recipients but also for its perpetrators.

The judgment for creating conflict and seeking to destroy a leader because of jealous ambition resulted in the governors and satraps forfeiting their own lives along with the lives of their wives and children. It was an enormous price to pay.

It remains so today. Those who seek to discredit a man of God, or any leader, because of selfish ambition and petty jealousy receive from God their just reward. They will ultimately be discovered for what they truly are and judged accordingly. They may not forfeit their lives, as those in Daniel's time, but God will judge them nevertheless.

As of this writing, the final results have yet to be determined regarding the accusations former Speaker of the House of Representatives Nancy Pelosi has leveled against the Central Intelligence Agency (CIA) regarding their failure to notify her and others members of Congress regarding the implementation of "water boarding" as a legitimate interrogation technique against terrorists during the presidency of George W. Bush. The CIA disputes her claim. The question remains, what did she know, and when did she know it? Who is telling the truth? Ultimately, one would expect the truth will be discovered and those compromising their integrity will be revealed.

The impact of Daniel's uncompromising character may have resulted in King Darius trusting God for his salvation as King Nebuchadnezzar before him (Daniel 4:1–3; 34–37, ESV). Evidence of this can be found in the king's own words:

> Then King Darius wrote to all the peoples, nations, and languages that dwell in all the earth: "Peace be multiplied to you. I make a decree, that in all my royal dominion people are to tremble and fear before the God of Daniel, for he is the living God, enduring forever; his kingdom shall never be destroyed, and his dominion shall be to the end. He delivers and rescues; he works signs and wonders in heaven and on earth, he who has saved Daniel from the power of the lions. (Daniel 6:25–27, ESV)

What follows is a postscript concerning Daniel: "So this Daniel prospered during the reign of Darius and the reign of Cyrus the Persian" (Daniel 6:28, ESV). From a youth to an elderly man, Daniel maintained consistency in his character. He would not compromise regardless of the circumstances of conflict he encountered.

For the believer today, the specific situations may vary and a leader may not encounter the exact same type of conflict as Daniel or other people. However, the principle of an uncompromising commitment to God and His word is the common thread which binds godly leaders together.

Following the conclusion of Judah's seventy year captivity, God led His people back to the land He had sworn to give them. The temple, destroyed by Babylon, was rebuilt (Ezra 1–3, ESV). Discouragements and conflicts were many, and soon, the work ceased. However, under the leadership of Zerubbabel, and with the help of the prophets Haggai and Zechariah, the work resumed (Ezra 5:1–2, ESV). In fact, Haggai displayed godly leadership when he proclaimed four messages (Haggai 1–2, ESV) whose total effect was to encourage the nation, its governor, and the remnant of the people to finish rebuilding the temple.

Ezra, "a skilled scribe in the Law of Moses" (Ezra 7:6, ESV) would lead many back to Jerusalem from Babylon and teach the statutes and ordinances of the Lord. The days were not easy, but Ezra was committed to overcome the conflict as much as he was committed to the word of God and to being a godly leader.

So too was Nehemiah, who followed Ezra some thirteen years later and who became responsible for rebuilding Jerusalem's walls. There was much opposition to the project but Nehemiah, and the people, persevered, and the walls were completed.

Between Ezra and Nehemiah, historically, was Queen Esther. The events chronicled in the book of Esther occurred between the first return of the Jews to Jerusalem under Zerubbabel and the second return that Ezra led. During this time, Queen Esther, the wife of the Persian King Ahasuerus, became a godly leader whom God used to protect Israel from the anti-Semitism of Haman the Agagite. Esther's story illustrates God's providential care of his people. The story of Esther shows how divine providence overrules all things.

Examining in detail some specific Old Testament characters, while surveying others, in no way should convey a demeaning or dismissing of the many godly men and women who encountered conflict and whom God used as His instruments prior to the New Testament. As the writer of Hebrews eloquently states:

> Women received back their dead by resurrection. Some were tortured, refusing to accept release, so that they might rise again to a better life. Others suffered mocking and flogging, and even chains and imprisonment. They were stoned, they were sawn in two, they were killed with the sword. They went about in skins of sheep and goats, destitute, afflicted, mistreated—of whom the world was not worthy—wandering about in deserts and mountains, and in dens and caves of the earth. (Hebrews 11:35–38, ESV)

These were men and women of faith. They were men and women who encountered conflict as they walked with God, but who stood tall and "of whom the world was not worthy" (Hebrews 11:38, ESV). These people anticipated the promise of God, fulfilled in the person of Jesus Christ and the salvation found only in Him.

The Wisdom literature of the Old Testament also contributes greatly to the subject of God developing godly leadership through conflict. This subject matter is found in the Psalms and Proverbs.

The Psalms are a collection of Hebrews songs, hymns, and poems taken from various periods in the history of Israel. There are 150 separate Psalms, and they are divided into five categories: hymns, community laments, royal psalms, thanksgiving psalms, and individual laments.

The individual lament psalms contain the prayers of persons in times of emergency, defeat, oppression, danger, or other similar conflicts. Psalm 22 (ESV) is an example. These psalms contain a cry for help, a confession of trust, a petition or plea, an appeal for God's care, a vow of praise, and an assurance of God's hearing. As authors LaSor, Hubbard, and Bush explain:

> Three types of circumstances seem to have prompted prayers of individual complaints: (1) unjust accusations of crime and wrongdoing, in which false witnesses conspired with enemies of the sufferer to convict and punish the defendant falsely; (2) penitence for personal sins; (3) illness or incapacity which at times seems to have been combined with unjust accusations. Whether the accusations made the sufferer ill or some illness led to accusations of sin, the sufferer is at once wracked with physical and emotional pain and abandoned by his loved ones. (LaSor, Hubbard, and Bush, 519)

The Psalms demonstrate that through life's conflicts God can be sought, petitioned, and trusted. It is also evident that through conflict, the psalmist grows in his relationship with God by trusting Him, relying upon Him, praising Him, resting in His mercy, guarding his own behavior, waiting upon Him, and hoping in Him. Additionally, the psalmist seeks God for refuge and strength, he rests in the Lord's goodness, he casts his burdens upon the Lord, and he cries for deliverance. The psalmist praises God for His faithfulness.

The book of Proverbs continues the theme of God developing godly leaders through conflict. The Proverbs are a collection of short statements teaching fundamental realities of life. They are principles for success rather than particular promises. Two major ideas contained in Proverbs are wisdom and folly.

God-ordained conflict, and man's response to it, is an ongoing subject in Proverbs. The statements contained therein point to man's relationship with God, his relationship to himself, and his relationship with others. Here are some examples from Proverbs regarding the godly leader's development through conflict.

- "Trust in the Lord with all your heart, and do not lean on your own understanding. In all your ways acknowledge him, and he will make straight your paths" (Proverbs 3:5–6, ESV).
- "My son, do not despise the Lord's discipline or be weary of his reproof, for the Lord reproves him whom he loves, as a father the son in whom he delights" (Proverbs 3:11–12, ESV).
- "Do not be afraid of sudden terror or of the ruin of the wicked, when it comes, for the Lord will be your confidence and will keep your foot from being caught" (Proverbs 3:25–26, ESV).

- "Do not envy a man of violence and do not choose any of his ways, for the devious person is an abomination to the Lord, but the upright are in his confidence. The Lord's curse is on the house of the wicked, but he blesses the dwelling of the righteous. Toward the scorners he is scornful, but to the humble he gives favor. The wise will inherit honor, but fools get disgrace" (Proverbs 3:31–35, ESV).
- "My son, keep your father's commandment, and forsake not your mother's teaching. Bind them on your heart always; tie them around your neck. When you walk, they will lead you; when you lie down, they will watch over you; and when you awake, they will talk with you. For the commandment is a lamp and the teaching a light, and the reproofs of discipline are the way of life" (Proverbs 6:20–23, ESV).
- "The fear of the Lord is the beginning of wisdom, and the knowledge of the Holy One is insight" (Proverbs 9:10, ESV).
- "The Lord does not let the righteous go hungry, but he thwarts the craving of the wicked" (Proverbs 10:3, ESV).
- "Whoever walks in integrity walks securely, but he who makes his ways crooked will be found out" (Proverbs 10:9, ESV).
- "When words are many, transgression is not lacking, but whoever restrains his lips is prudent" (Proverbs 10:19, ESV).
- "The simple believes everything, but the prudent gives thought to his steps. One who is wise is cautious and turns away from evil, but a fool is reckless and careless. A man of quick temper acts foolishly, and a man of evil devices is hated. The simple inherit folly, but the prudent are

crowned with knowledge. The evil bow down before the good, the wicked at the gates of the righteous" (Proverbs 14:15–19, ESV).

- "A hot-tempered man stirs up strife, but he who is slow to anger quiets contention" (Proverbs 15:18, ESV).
- "Commit your work to the LORD, and your plans will be established" (Proverbs 16:3, ESV).
- "The crucible is for silver, and the furnace is for gold, and the LORD tests hearts" (Proverbs 17:3, ESV).
- "The beginning of strife is like letting out water, so quit before the quarrel breaks out" (Proverbs 17:14, ESV).
- "Whoever isolates himself seeks his own desire; he breaks out against all sound judgment" (Proverbs 18:1, ESV).
- "An intelligent heart acquires knowledge, and the ear of the wise seeks knowledge" (Proverbs 18:15, ESV).
- "It is an honor for a man to keep aloof from strife, but every fool will be quarreling. The sluggard does not plow in the autumn; he will seek at harvest and have nothing. The purpose in a man's heart is like deep water, but a man of understanding will draw it out. Many a man proclaims his own steadfast love, but a faithful man who can find? The righteous who walks in his integrity—blessed are his children after him" (Proverbs 20:3–7, ESV).
- "Do not say, 'I will repay evil'; wait for the LORD, and he will deliver you. Unequal weights are an abomination to the LORD, and false scales are not good. A man's steps are from the LORD; how then can man understand his way" (Proverbs 20:22–24, ESV).
- "Every way of a man is right in his own eyes, but the LORD weighs the heart. To do righteousness and justice is more acceptable to the LORD than sacrifice" (Proverbs 21:2–3, ESV).

- "No wisdom, no understanding, no counsel can avail against the Lord. The horse is made ready for the day of battle, but the victory belongs to the Lord" (Proverbs 21:30–31, ESV).
- "The eyes of the Lord keep watch over knowledge, but he overthrows the words of the traitor" (Proverbs 22:12, ESV).
- "Apply your heart to instruction and your ear to words of knowledge" (Proverbs 23:12, ESV).
- "If you faint in the day of adversity, your strength is small" (Proverbs 24:10, ESV).
- "Do not rejoice when your enemy falls, and let not your heart be glad when he stumbles, lest the Lord see it and be displeased, and turn away his anger from him. Fret not yourself because of evildoers, and be not envious of the wicked, (Proverbs 24:17–19; Proverbs 24:20, ESV).
- "A word fitly spoken is like apples of gold in a setting of silver. Like a gold ring or an ornament of gold is a wise reprover to a listening ear" (Proverbs 25:11–12, ESV).

It is evident that Proverbs has much to offer regarding God developing godly leadership through conflict. However, the theme of God using conflict to develop leaders is not only weaved throughout the fabric of the Old Testament but also in the New Testament. This pattern is found throughout the gospels, the historical narrative, the epistles, and the apocalyptic literature. Wise is the leader who familiarizes himself with the predominant material contained in the New Testament concerning the development of godly leadership through conflict.

CHAPTER THREE

The Theological and Biblical Issues of Conflict: New Testament Examples

When God took on human form in the person of Jesus Christ, He was not immune to conflict in this world. Rather, Jesus encountered difficulties throughout His life, up to and including His death on the cross. As the New Testament begins, the four gospels clearly demonstrate and articulate this truth. From His birth until His substitutionary death, Jesus was indeed "despised and rejected by men; a man of sorrows, and acquainted with grief; and as one from whom men hide their faces he was despised, and we esteemed him not" (Isaiah 53:3, ESV).

Whether it was King Herod who sought to take Jesus's life following the visit by the Magi, the intense temptations from Satan while in the wilderness, the increasing animosity of the religious leaders, the debates following Jesus's miracles including His healing on the Sabbath, the efforts by the Pharisees to kill Jesus, or the events immediately preceding and including the crucifixion, the Lord's life contained continual conflict. In placing these events in context, Hebrews 5:5–8 (ESV) states:

> So also Christ did not glorify Himself to become High Priest, but it was He who said to Him: You are My Son, today I have begotten You. As He also says in another place: You are a priest forever according to the order of Melchizedek; Who (Christ) in the days of His flesh, when He offered up prayers and supplications, with vehement cries and tears to Him who was able to save Him from death, and was heard, because of His godly fear, though He was a Son, yet He learned obedience by the things which He suffered.

When the writer of Hebrews said that Christ "learned obedience by the things which He suffered" (Hebrews 5:8, ESV), he was not implying that Christ lacked anything in His incarnated existence to be supplied by either conflicting or suffering situations. Christ did not need to suffer in order to conquer or correct any disobedience. His suffering demonstrated that He was, is, and always will be the sinless, second person of the Godhead. There was no suggestion in His conflicts that He would succumb to the temptations and trials He endured, but that He would always be obedient to the Father. Therefore, His righteous life was the necessary prerequisite for His subsitutionary death for sinners.

He humbled Himself in His humanity in order to learn. Philippians 2:8 (ESV) says that "and being found in human form, he humbled himself by becoming obedient to the point of death, even death on a cross." It was through the experiences of suffering and conflict, the climatic episode being the cross, that Christ, in His humanity learned obedience.

Therefore, because Jesus encountered and withstood conflict, He is able to not only sympathize with us when we encounter struggles but also provide the necessary strength and ability to overcome those difficulties and become better leaders because of them.

Additionally, Hebrews 2:18 (ESV) states that "for because he himself has suffered when tempted, he is able to help those who are being tempted." The conflicts Jesus encountered when He faced temptations not only evidence His genuine humanity but also His ability to sympathize and understand the temptations and conflicts godly leaders encounter.

Peter gives believers another benefit to glean from the conflict Jesus endured on this earth. In 1 Peter 2:11–25 (ESV), the apostle instructed his readers in the importance of living in the world with an attitude of submission. Peter realized that even when believers submit to the government and servants submit to their masters, Christians may suffer wrongfully. When this happens, God gives His children clear instructions in how to respond:

> For what credit is it if, when you sin and are beaten for it, you endure? But if when you do good and suffer for it you endure, this is a gracious thing in the sight of God. For to this you have been called, because Christ also suffered for you, leaving you an example, so that you might follow in his steps. He committed no sin, neither was deceit found in his mouth. When he was reviled, he did not revile in return; when he suffered, he did not threaten, but continued entrusting himself to him who judges justly. (1 Peter 2:20–23, ESV)

In following Jesus's example when facing conflict, godly leaders are (1) to make sure their suffering is because of the good they have done, (2) to face conflict with patience, (3) to not revile when reviled, (4) to not threaten, and (5) to commit themselves to God the Father who judges righteously. When individuals handle conflict, as Jesus did, this is commendable before God and it develops them into the godly leaders God desires.

In fact, Jesus's final words to the disciples during the Upper Room Discourse were as follows: "I have said these things to you, that in me you may have peace. In the world you will have tribulation. But take heart; I have overcome the world" (John 16:33, ESV). What was true for those disciples in that immediate context is also true for Jesus's disciples today.

After Jesus's resurrection and ascension, the church became a reality (Acts 2, ESV). It should not be surprising that as the church grew, so did conflict within the church. It is naïveté for the church leader to imagine that conflict will be absent from a congregation. It is a wise leader who anticipates conflict as a necessary eventuality rather than an inconvenient possibility. What conflicts did the early church experience and what leadership qualities did God develop in those early church leaders?

In Matthew 18:15–35 (ESV), Jesus spoke to His disciples concerning the subject of church discipline and the ultimate restoration of a Christian brother who sins against another Christian. Throughout Jesus's instructions about church discipline (vs. 15–20), His answer to Peter's question concerning how many times an offended party should forgive (vs 21–22), and His subsequent illustration about an unforgiving steward (vs. 23–35), Jesus focused on the leadership quality of forgiveness.

When conflict occurs in the church, the chief aim of leadership should be repentance by, and restoration of, the offending party with forgiveness extended by all throughout the exchange. This also applies to the pastor, who not only should seek forgiveness, when and where appropriate, but who should also be forgiving.

When Ananias and Sapphira lied to God and the church about how much they received from the sale of a parcel of property, the judgment of God was quick and severe, they both died (Acts 5:1–11, ESV). The text clearly indicates their death was the result of God's judgment. The text says that "great fear came upon the whole church and upon all who heard of these things" (Acts 5:11, ESV).

Conflict prompts godly leaders to fear God greatly. The context of Acts 5 indicates that the fear spoken of was not just dread or terror, but also a reverential fear. This was a fear "of God as a controlling motive of life, in matters spiritual and moral, not a mere "fear" of His power and righteous retribution, but a wholesome dread of displeasing Him" (Vine, 230). God permits conflict so godly leaders will reverence and please Him.

In Acts 6:1–7 (ESV), the church conflict in question was the failure to give equal treatment to the Hellenistic widows (Acts 6:1, ESV). The reason for this oversight may have been because the church was growing, or it could have been an incident of cultural prejudice. The twelve apostles resolved the conflict when they summoned the church and commissioned them to select godly men who were to oversee the food distribution (Acts 6:3, ESV). This enabled the apostles to attend to their responsibilities of prayer and the ministry of the word (Acts 6:4, ESV).

Conflict prompts godly leaders to address problems and to seek solutions. This may be by direct involvement and/or delegation of responsibilities. Either way, a godly leader must address the issues affecting a church and initiate practical and biblical means to solve the problems.

By Acts 8 (ESV), church conflict was in full force. The historical context was the immediate aftermath of Stephen's martyrdom. A young man name Saul "approved of his execution" (Acts 8:1, ESV). The martyrdom resulted in a great persecution arising against the church at Jerusalem. Believers, except the apostles, scattered throughout Judea and Samaria to avoid arrest. Saul began attacking Christians and placing them in prison because of their efforts to share the gospel.

A direct result of this persecution was the gospel began to be preached in other areas, such as Samaria. Phillip preached Christ to the city of Samaria and "the crowds with one accord paid attention to what was being said by Philip when they heard him and saw the signs that he did" (Acts 8:6, ESV). The demon-possessed were delivered, and many who were paralyzed and lame were healed. God used conflict to create opportunities for spreading the gospel.

At this time, a man called Simon, who was a sorcerer (Acts 8:9–12, ESV), believed the gospel which Philip preached. Simon not only believed but was also baptized. However, he soon sought to buy the ability to lay hands upon people so they would receive the Holy Spirit.

Whether Simon truly understood the significance of his actions is debatable, but Peter certainly did. He pronounced judgment by stating "May your silver perish with you, because you thought you could obtain the gift of God with money! You have neither part nor lot in this matter, for your heart is not right before God" (Acts 8:20–21, ESV). Peter added, "Repent, therefore, of this wickedness of yours, and pray to the Lord that, if possible, the intent of your heart may be forgiven you. For I see that you are in the gall of bitterness and in the bond of iniquity" (Acts 8:22–23, ESV). As a godly leader, Peter would not accommodate inappropriate behavior or false doctrine. He confronted the immature and dangerous theology of Simon in no uncertain terms.

It was sometime after this that the Holy Spirit came upon the Gentiles at Cornelius's household through Peter's preaching (Acts 10, ESV). Non-Jews were receiving the word of God (Acts 11:1, ESV). However, Jewish Christians contented with Peter when he returned to Jerusalem saying, "You went to uncircumcised men and ate with them" (Acts 11:3, ESV). The word "contend" means to "dispute and to separate" (Kittel, 474).

Peter's response in this conflict was Spirit controlled and biblical. He explained the circumstances which occurred in Acts 10 (ESV) and concluded that "if then God gave the same gift to them as he gave to us when we believed in the Lord Jesus Christ, who was I that I could stand in God's way?" (Acts 11:17, ESV).

Confronting the argumentative with God's truth resulted in the people becoming silent. They then began glorifying God by saying. "Then to the Gentiles also God has granted repentance that leads to life" (Acts 11:18, ESV). However, the issue would continue to fester resulting in the Jerusalem Council (Acts 15:1–35, ESV).

Conflict reached a fever pitch in the early church at Antioch concerning the nature of true, saving faith. There were individuals who were teaching that unless you became a Jew through the ritual of circumcision, then you could not become a Christian. Would a Gentile have to become a Jew in order to be a Christian? Paul and Barnabas encountered a great dispute over this subject. The contention was so great that the Antiochian church determined that Paul and Barnabas and some of the others be appointed to "go up to Jerusalem to the apostles and the elders about this question" (Acts 15:2, ESV).

The debate continued once the pair reached Jerusalem. There were Pharisees who argued that it was "necessary to circumcise them and to order them to keep the Law of Moses" (Acts 15:5, ESV). In the midst of this conflict, the apostles and elders met to consider the matter.

In debating whether salvation was by grace alone, through faith alone, in Christ alone, Peter stood and related how God directed him to preach to the Gentiles and that God "made no distinction between us and them, having cleansed their hearts by faith" (Acts 15:9, ESV). These were bold words in an emotionally heated environment, but Peter was not finished.

He continued by saying, "Now, therefore, why are you putting God to the test by placing a yoke on the neck of the disciples that neither our fathers nor we have been able to bear? But we believe that we will be saved through the grace of the Lord Jesus, just as they will" (Acts 15:10–11, ESV). Peter would not compromise from the true nature of salvation being all of God. God uses conflict to maintain the purity of the gospel.

Paul and Barnabas reiterated their experiences of God's miraculous verification of salvation among the Gentiles (Acts 15:12, ESV). James then decreed, on the basis of Peter's testimony and the biblical text of Amos 9:11–12 (ESV), "that we should not trouble those of the Gentiles who turn to God, but should write to them to abstain from the things polluted by idols, and from sexual immorality, and from what has been strangled, and from blood" (Acts 15:19–20, ESV).

The result was a unity of spirit among the entire church. The leaders refused to compromise the biblical truth regarding the nature of saving faith in order to placate a vocal minority. Within the church today, godly leaders must do the same.

The conflict seen in Acts 15:36–41 (ESV) is one which happens all too often in a church: leaders disagreeing with each other resulting in estranged friendships. Paul and Barnabas agreed they needed to revisit the churches where they previously preached the Word of God. What they did not agree on was whether John-Mark should accompany them.

Paul was adamant that Mark should not join them because he had deserted the team during the First Missionary Journey. Yet Barnabas was equally determined to again include John-Mark. The resulting contention was so sharp between Paul and Barnabas "so that they separated from each other. Barnabas took Mark with him and sailed away to Cyprus" (Acts 15:39, ESV).

Although Paul and Barnabas eventually reconciled and Paul would later count Mark as "useful to me for ministry" (2 Timothy 4:11, ESV), theirs was not an amicable parting. The weight of evidence seems to favor Paul, since he was an apostle, and the church in Antioch commended both he and Silas to God's grace when they departed for Syria and Cilicia. There was no similar commendation for Barnabas and Mark when they sailed to Cyprus.

What can we learn from this conflict between two brothers in Christ? First, mutual submission should be in force (Ephesians 5:21, ESV), and neither side should seek to enforce its will when the issue, as it was with Mark, is a judgment call with no obvious right or wrong answer. Second, such a disagreement should never reach the point of intensity as it did with Paul and Barnabas. Finally, all parties should recognize the sovereignty of God, in that He causes all things to work together for good (Romans 8:28, NASB). In the context, instead of one missionary team traveling, there were two. God uses conflict to accomplish a greater goal.

Conflict was also a companion of Paul at the conclusion of his ministry. As Paul neared the end of his Third Missionary Journey, he shared some final thoughts with the Ephesian church elders before he embarked for Jerusalem (Acts 20:17–38, ESV). It was a tender moment, for both Paul and the church leaders realized that they would probably not see each other alive again (Acts 20:25, ESV).

Paul anticipated conflict in the church because of false teachers who would speak "twisted things, to draw away the disciples after them" (Acts 20:30, ESV).He commanded the elders to "pay careful attention to yourselves and to all the flock, in which the Holy Spirit has made you overseers, to care for the church of God, which he obtained with his own blood" (Acts 20:28, ESV) and to "therefore be alert, remembering that for three years I did not cease night or day to admonish every one with tears" (Acts 20:31, ESV). Godly leaders can never let their guard down in protecting the congregation they oversee.

Church conflict often occurs due to disagreements concerning issues that are not expressly right or wrong. Many a church split has occurred because of what side of the platform the church piano should be on or whether there should be carpet or tile in the auditorium. Romans 14 (ESV) address the principles of how to handle these types of issues.

The primary attitude godly leaders should demonstrate when encountering conflict of this nature is a nonjudgmental spirit (vs. 10–12). A leader should not take sides, but rather ensure neither side condemns nor judges the other (vs. 1–3).

A godly leader should also be ready to relinquish the right to participate in an activity if such participation causes a fellow believer to stumble (vs. 13). The leader must "pursue what makes for peace and for mutual upbuilding" (Romans 14:19, ESV). As the pastor demonstrates his willingness to submit to the principles of Romans 14 (ESV), he sets an excellent standard for the congregation. The pastor cannot expect the congregation to follow this example if he is not leading by example.

In addressing contentious people in the church, Romans 16:17–18 (ESV) says, "I appeal to you, brothers, to watch out for those who cause divisions and create obstacles contrary to the doctrine that you have been taught; avoid them. For such persons do not serve our Lord Christ, but their own appetites, and by smooth talk and flattery they deceive the hearts of the naïve" (Romans 16:17–18, ESV).

Pastors must know when to watch for people within, and outside, the congregation seeking to propagate conflict. This may not be easy, or understood, but it is biblical. Avoiding these individuals means to "turn away," which is from the Greek word "ἐκκλίνω" (*eklino*). This is a command that the believer is to actively and continually obey. "Paul did not say 'oppose them' for, though some of those whom he addresses might have been able to do this successfully, others could easily have been led astray if they had entered into a debate. Therefore Paul urged the brothers to avoid these dissenters altogether" (Hendrickson, 510).

The reason for such a command is that such people are filled with their own self-importance and are unwilling to submit to the clear teachings of Scripture. They are flatterers, hedonists, and deceivers. When this form of conflict arises, the pastoral leader shows wisdom by not engaging in any debate with such people.

Often conflict in the local church occurs because people in the congregation favor one pastor over another. One pastor can do no right while another can do no wrong. How should pastors lead when this type of conflict occurs?

1 Corinthians 1:10–17 (ESV) explains that sectarianism occurred in the church at Corinth, and Paul would not tolerate it. He emphasized the unity of the Spirit, and he pleaded with the Corinthian church that "by the name of our Lord Jesus Christ, that all of you agree, and that there be no divisions among you, but that you be united in the same mind and the same judgment."

Meanwhile, additional problems arose. A young man was having an affair with his father's wife (1 Corinthians 5:1–13, ESV). The church failed to deal with this behavior, but Paul did not hesitate to confront the church for its unwillingness to address immorality (1 Corinthians 5:1–2, ESV). He instructed the church to deliver the perpetrator "to Satan for the destruction of the flesh, so that his spirit may be saved in the day of the Lord" (1 Corinthians 5:5, ESV). Paul displayed a determination to judge unrepentant sin in the church rather than permit it to continue (1 Corinthians 5:6–13, ESV).

Another problem facing the Corinthian church involved believers taking other believers to court (1 Corinthians 6:1–8, ESV). Paul challenged them to find godly men to settle the dispute and to perhaps accept injustice rather than "go to law against one another."

1 Corinthians 7:1–40 (ESV) chronicled Paul's response to several questions regarding widowhood, marriage, remarriage, and singleness. Throughout the discourse, Paul spoke rationally, thoroughly, and biblically concerning the practical solutions to tough issues affecting believers so that there would be no resulting conflict because of misunderstanding or misinformation.

1 Corinthians 8:1–13 (ESV) mirrors the debate found in Romans 14 concerning debatable issues. Paul displayed a willingness to set aside his personal freedom in Christ if it resulted in another believer not stumbling in their faith (1 Corinthians 8:13, ESV).

Paul addressed male and female roles in the church in 1 Corinthians 11:3–16 (ESV) and unsuitable behavior when observing the Lord's Supper (1 Corinthians 11:17–34, ESV). Like Paul, a godly leader must engage the church in honest discussions regarding culture and local customs, with Scripture as the standard for behavior and practice.

The concluding controversy in 1 Corinthians dealt with worship and whether it was appropriate to speak in tongues (1 Corinthians 14:26-40 ESV). Displaying the same love he spoke of in chapter thirteen, Paul instructed the church regarding how it should conduct its worship services. Without any haughtiness, Paul clearly set down principles for corporate gatherings highlighting edification as the ultimate goal.

Continuing through the New Testament, God's instructions concerning godly leadership are conspicuously seen in 2 Corinthians (ESV). Throughout this epistle, the Apostle Paul lists the behavior traits pastoral leaders acquire through conflict and must evidence in ministry:

- The leader is to not lose heart, to renounce the hidden things of shame, to not walk in craftiness nor handle the word of God deceitfully, to manifest the truth, and to commend oneself to every man's conscience (2 Corinthians 4:1–2, ESV).
- The pastor is to display humility by preaching Christ Jesus the Lord and oneself as a bondservant (2 Corinthians 4:5, ESV) and to recognize that believers are clay pots in which God has entrusted the glorious treasure of the gospel (2 Corinthians 4:7, ESV).
- The godly leader's aim is to please the Lord regardless of the circumstances (2 Corinthians 5:9; 6:3–10, ESV).
- The pastor must cleanse himself from all filthiness of the flesh and spirit, to strive to be holy and to have a reverential fear of God (2 Corinthians 7:1, ESV).
- The godly leader is to know that God will comfort him while he is in the midst of conflict (2 Corinthians 7:5–7, ESV).
- The pastor is to complete the task God has given to him (2 Corinthians 8:10–11, ESV).
- The godly leader must recognize that spiritual conflict must be fought with spiritual weapons (2 Corinthians 10:1–6, ESV).
- The pastor must not boast in another man's accomplishments but rather seek to be commended by the Lord (2 Corinthians 10:16–18, ESV).
- The godly leader can boast only in his infirmity (2 Corinthians 11:16–30, ESV).

- The pastor must know that God's grace is sufficient (2 Corinthians 12:7–10, ESV).

The epistle to the Galatians gives three examples of leadership developed through conflict. Paul was bold to confront a fellow apostle when Peter evidenced hypocrisy (Galatians 2:1–16, ESV), and he acknowledged that suffering was a clear indication that he was preaching the gospel: the offense of the cross. He also indicated that when conflict arises with another brother in Christ, the spiritual are to restore this one in a spirit of gentleness and to bear one another's burdens (Galatians 5:26–6:5, ESV).

In Ephesians, Paul stated that godly leaders should "walk in a manner worthy of the calling to which you have been called, with all humility and gentleness, with patience, bearing with one another in love, eager to maintain the unity of the Spirit in the bond of peace" (Ephesians 4:1–3, ESV).The circumstances of conflict will enhance a leader's character.

Additionally, the godly leader must not permit any corrupt word to proceed out of his mouth, but only edifying speech that "it may give grace to those who hear" (Ephesians 4:29, ESV). When hurt by conflict, the leader must not let bitterness, wrath, clamor, evil speaking, and malice be a part of his life but rather kindness, tenderheartedness, and forgiveness (Ephesians 4:31–32, ESV).

There have been times when I, and my family, have been hurt by people within the church. I pray that I have never been the cause of pain within the congregation. However, whenever hurts occur, the recipient is never to become embittered.

One way a leader can strive for the disciplines mentioned in Ephesians is by following the instructions in Philippians 2:1–4 (ESV). Through the consolation, comfort, affection, mercy, and fellowship with Christ, pastors are to let nothing be done through selfish ambition or conceit, but in humility, let each esteem others better than himself. Hard feelings, which could be formed through conflict, should be supplanted by an attitude of lowliness and humility and a genuine concern for others. Our supreme example is Jesus Christ (Philippians 2:5–11, ESV).

Godly leaders must do "all things without grumbling or disputing" (Philippians 2:14, ESV). The reason is to be a child of God that is "blameless and innocent…without blemish in the midst of a crooked and twisted generation, among whom you shine as lights in the world" (Philippians 2:15, ESV).The failure to do so results in a poor testimony like Euodia and Syntyche whom Paul urged "to agree in the Lord" (Philippians 4:2, ESV).

The Church at Colosse had similar conflicts. People were judging each other's spirituality based on outward appearances and personal preferences (Colossians 2:16–23, ESV). Paul encouraged them to strive for true godliness which resides in one's heartfelt affection for God (Colossians 3:1–4:6, ESV). The godly perspective for all believers was that "whatever you do, in word or deed, do everything in the name of the Lord Jesus, giving thanks to God the Father through him" (Colossians 3:17, ESV).

In 1 Thessalonians 4:6–8 (ESV) Paul addressed the issue of sexual immorality. Not only did he instruct believers to abstain from such behavior, but also that godly leaders must "aspire to live quietly, and to mind your own affairs, and to work with your hands, as we instructed you, so that you may walk properly before outsiders and be dependent on no one" (1 Thessalonians 4:11–12, ESV).

These thoughts are reiterated in 2 Thessalonians 3:6–15 (ESV) where Paul set an example for believers to follow by financially supporting himself through hard work night and day. There were disorderly people in the church and they were lazy and irresponsible.

Paul's answer to this church conflict was not just commanding fellow believers to withdraw themselves from the habitually irresponsible (2 Thessalonians 3:6, ESV), but he also displayed godly leadership by setting an example of hard work and responsibility (2 Thessalonians 3:10–12, ESV). A leader must not only teach correct doctrine, he must also live the doctrine he teaches.

When Paul wrote Timothy an initial letter, his young protégé was embroiled in church conflict at Ephesus. False doctrine was being taught by those causing disputes in the church (1 Timothy 1:3-4 ESV). Paul described these false teachers as having "wandered away into vain discussion" (1 Timothy 1:6, ESV).

Paul urged Timothy not to accommodate these people but rather fight them by having a strong commitment to the truth of the gospel and by having a good conscience by obedience to God's truth (1 Timothy 1:19 ESV). By doing so, he would not be like others who "having rejected, concerning the faith, have suffered shipwreck." Paul encouraged Timothy to earn his congregation's respect by setting a good example. He said, "Let no one despise you for your youth, but set the believers an example in speech, in conduct, in love, in faith, in purity" (1 Timothy 4:12, ESV).

Furthermore, Paul urged him to maintain a strong commitment to God's word and to "devote yourself to the public reading of Scripture, to exhortation, to teaching" (1 Timothy 4:13, ESV). He also told Timothy to "not neglect the gift you have, which was given you by prophecy when the council of elders laid their hands on you" (1 Timothy 4:14, ESV).

Additionally, Paul challenged the young pastor to "practice these things, immerse yourself in them, so that all may see your progress" (1 Timothy 4:15, ESV). Progress, from "προκοπή" (*prokopa*), "denotes moral and spiritual development, cultural progress, or advance in virtue" (Kittel, 939). The conflict Timothy faced, as pastors and leaders today are facing, resulted in a moral and spiritual development unattainable by comfort and ease. The development of human muscles requires the increasing resistance of greater weight. The development of a leader of character requires the increasing resistance of great conflict.

Depending on what individuals were creating conflict, Paul counseled Timothy to follow God ordained guidelines when confronting people in the church. He said to "not rebuke an older man but encourage him as you would a father, younger men as brothers, older women as mothers, younger women as sisters, in all purity" (1 Timothy 5:1–2, ESV).

Paul did not deny the reality of conflict, nor did he tell Timothy to run from it. Rather, he gave his young son in the faith practical instructions for how to act when facing conflict. The goal would be for the church to see Timothy's progress as a godly leader. Paul gave similar instructions to Titus in Titus 1:10–11(ESV) and 3:9–11 (ESV).

The Epistle to the Hebrews contributes the significant principle of endurance to the subject of God using conflict to develop godly leadership. In Hebrews 10:32–39 (ESV) the writer encourages the Hebrew Christians to endure in their faith in spite of persecutions because of their faith.

An effective way to fortify people against future trials is to remind them of the courage they displayed in past trials. This is precisely what the writer of Hebrews did. His readers knew what it was to stand their ground in a great contest in the face of suffering.

The writer of Hebrews continues his exhortation regarding endurance during conflict in chapter 12:1–11 (ESV). Following the examples of faith by Old Testament saints, the writer encouraged his readers to persevere by using the metaphor of a runner. "Therefore, since we are surrounded by so great a cloud of witnesses, let us also lay aside every weight, and sin which clings so closely, and let us run with endurance the race that is set before us" (Hebrews 12:1, ESV).

A Christian, and especially a leader, must discipline themselves to put off every sin in their life. As a recreational runner who has participated in several 5K, 10K, and 25K races, I have learned that the lightest and most basic clothing is necessary to compete successfully. Too much clothing can weigh you down and sap your strength the further you are in your run. This is especially true during warm weather.

The same can be said for the believer who is running the race of godliness. Sin weighs us down with guilt. Continual and intimate fellowship is necessary to persevere. God will use conflict to purify us from weighted sin.

The believer's example in running the race is none other than Jesus Christ. Christians are to keep "looking to Jesus, the founder and perfecter of our faith, who for the joy that was set before him endured the cross, despising the shame, and is seated at the right hand of the throne of God" (Hebrews 12:2, ESV). Jesus persevered so that He would receive the joy of accomplishing the Father's will (Hebrews 1:9 ESV; Psalm 16:9–11 ESV; Luke 10:21–24, ESV). As godly leaders today encounter conflict, they are to persevere so that they also receive the joy of accomplishing the Father's will.

In Hebrews 12:3 (ESV), the writer continued to urge his readers to "consider him who endured from sinners such hostility against himself, so that you may not grow weary or fainthearted" (Hebrews 12:3, ESV). Jesus is our supreme example of One willing to suffer in obedience to God. All who follow Him face the same opposition. See Acts 28:22 (ESV), Galatians 6:17 (ESV), Colossians 1:24 (ESV), and 2 Timothy 3:12 (ESV).

However, they did not encounter conflict resulting in death. While there were exceptions, the Hebrews had "not yet resisted to the point of shedding your blood" (Hebrews 12:4, ESV). Besides endurance, what was a further purpose God had in the conflict the Hebrews encountered?

It is at this moment that the writer of Hebrews quotes from Proverbs 3:11–12 (ESV). "And have you forgotten the exhortation that addresses you as sons? 'My son, do not regard lightly the discipline of the Lord, nor be weary when reproved by him. For the Lord disciplines the one he loves, and chastises every son whom he receives'" (Hebrews 12:5–6, ESV). God uses conflict to educate and discipline believers. Rather than evidencing God's hatred, trials, and sufferings display God's love for His children. In fact, the text continues by saying that "if you are left without discipline, in which all have participated, then you are illegitimate children and not sons" (Hebrews 12:8, ESV).

God desires to save and conform us "to the image of His Son" (Romans 8.29b, ESV). This conformity to Jesus Christ occurs one way through God chastening leaders through conflicts, trials, and difficulties. As believer's earthly fathers disciplined them to be submissive to his will, so much more so will their heavenly Father discipline them so they will be submissive to His will (Hebrews 12:9—10, ESV). While the discipline believers received from their earthly father was imperfect, God's discipline is eternal, perfect, and always for the purpose of holiness.

The conflict God brings into the leader's life, and the resulting chastening, is painful, regardless of when and where the leader encounters it. However, after the conflict is over, "it yields the peaceful fruit of righteousness to those who have been trained by it" (Hebrews 12:11, ESV).

I have learned this painful, but necessary, lesson. However, a friend of mine is in the midst of learning this lesson from the Lord. He is hurting. He and his wife are struggling to understand why a church plant, God directed them to begin, fractured into a split congregation resulting in its closing. He is in the midst of the training. I hope that soon he will evidence the fruit of righteousness from God through this time of instruction.

Conflict and trials change godly leaders. That is God's intended outcome. While some emerge from a conflict bitter and angry, God's ultimate purpose is a refinement of righteousness. God desires godly leaders who are holy, and leaders must realize that conflicts will occur in order to make them more holy. This theology of leadership through conflict continues in the Epistle of James.

James begins his epistle with the subject of conflict and what the leader's attitude should be when encountering difficulties. "Count it all joy, my brothers, when you meet trials of various kinds, for you know that the testing of your faith produces steadfastness. And let steadfastness have its full effect, that you may be perfect and complete, lacking in nothing" (James 1:2–4, ESV). The leader's attitude when conflict comes should be joy. A more complete explanation of this passage is contained in chapter three.

Additional leadership qualities that God develops include being "quick to hear, slow to speak, slow to anger" (James 1:19, ESV). Maintaining control over one's tongue (James 3:1–14, ESV) is not only wise counsel in tranquility but also in conflict.

When facing conflict, the godly leader must discern the spiritual battle being fought. Certain acceptable attitudes and actions easily embraced in our present culture must be identified for what they truly are—satanic. While they may encounter them, leaders must never have bitter envy and self-seeking in their heart. This wisdom is "earthly, unspiritual, demonic" (James 3:15b, ESV). "For where jealousy and selfish ambition exist, there will be disorder and every vile practice" (James 3:16, ESV). Therefore, what attitudes does James believe a godly leader must possess?

James explains that the godly individual should possess wisdom from God which is "pure, then peaceable, gentle, open to reason, full of mercy and good fruits, impartial and sincere"

(James 3:17, ESV). James explains that "a harvest of righteousness is sown in peace by those who make peace" (James 3:18, ESV). Therefore, the leader should seek to be a peacemaker at all times, especially in conflict.

James further states that conflict occurs when people do not get what they want. James asks:

> What causes quarrels and what causes fights among you? Is it not this, that your passions are at war within you? You desire and do not have, so you murder. You covet and cannot obtain, so you fight and quarrel. You do not have, because you do not ask. You ask and do not receive, because you ask wrongly, to spend it on your passions. (James 4:1–3, ESV)

In the midst of this kind of turmoil, godly leaders are not to speak evil of other Christians. "The one who speaks against a brother or judges his brother, speaks evil against the law and judges the law. But if you judge the law, you are not a doer of the law but a judge" (James 4:11, ESV). Additionally, believers are not to "grumble against one another, brothers, so that you may not be judged; behold, the Judge is standing at the door" (James 5:9, ESV). Once again, the tongue is described as a paramount area God seeks to master in the leader's life through conflict.

Peter also contributes to the discussion of leaders growing through various trials in his two epistles. He encourages the recipients of his first letter to recognize that God purposes conflict for a reason: "so that the tested genuineness of your faith—more precious than gold that perishes though it is tested by fire—may be found to result in praise and glory and honor at the revelation of Jesus Christ" (1 Peter 1:7, ESV). God allows conflict so the godly leader's faith will be tested, and he will glorify God. Peter continues to say that trials should not surprise us. We should expect them, learn from them, and know how to behave in the midst of them.

> Beloved, do not be surprised at the fiery trial when it comes upon you to test you, as though something strange were happening to you. But rejoice insofar as you share Christ's sufferings, that you may also rejoice and be glad when his glory is revealed. If you are insulted for the name of Christ, you are blessed, because the Spirit of glory and of God rests upon you. But let none of you suffer as a murderer or a thief or an evildoer or as a meddler. Yet if anyone suffers as a Christian, let him not be ashamed, but let him glorify God in that name. (1 Peter 4:12–16, ESV)

Much like Paul's encouragement to Timothy, Peter exhorts the elders among his readers to be good examples of Christ-likeness. He states that they are to "shepherd the flock of God that is among you, exercising oversight, not under compulsion, but willingly, as God would have you; not for shameful gain, but eagerly; not domineering over those in your charge, but being examples to the flock" (1 Peter 5:1–3, ESV).

In Peter's second epistle, the apostle extensively addresses the issue of false teachers and the resulting conflict they bring to the church. He concludes his letter by encouraging the leaders to be steadfast, not to embrace error, and to "grow in the grace and knowledge of our Lord and Savior Jesus Christ. To him be the glory both now and to the day of eternity. Amen" (2 Peter 3:18, ESV).

The Apostle John encourages leaders to "not imitate evil but imitate good. Whoever does good is from God; whoever does evil has not seen God" (3 John 1:11, ESV). The reasoning is because he who does good is of God, but he who does evil has not seen God. A godly leader must be a good role model for a congregation.

The godly leader being a good role model for those who follow him became practically evident for a good friend of mine. He was accused of having an affair with a coworker. The accusation was not true, but that did not stop the person responsible for the charge from continuing to accuse my friend.

When the situation eventually resulted in a meeting moderated by an outside mediator, my friend was exonerated of all charges. The woman responsible for the accusations admitted to being jealous over the working relationship this man had with other employees but not with her. She expressed contrition and sorrow for the pain she caused.

Throughout the ordeal, lasting several months, my friend's conduct, before, during, and after, was an example of courage under fire and graciousness under pressure. When others urged him to lash out at his accuser, he refrained. When he could have easily made her work life miserable after the mediation was completed, he did not. He displayed the utmost kindness and understanding. The other employees witnessed that his character of speech was supported by his character of life. This was because he was committed to studying and applying God's word.

Jude urges leaders to maintain their personal relationship with God by "building yourselves up in your most holy faith and praying in the Holy Spirit, keep yourselves in the love of God, waiting for the mercy of our Lord Jesus Christ that leads to eternal life" (Jude 20–21, ESV). He further states that when leaders encounter people who create conflict in the church, they should have compassion on some and preach the gospel to others (Jude 22–23, ESV).

The Revelation of Jesus Christ concludes the biblical canon. There are many rich theological themes contained in John's inspired text, including the exhortation for believers to reject sin and pursue holiness while in the midst of spiritual conflict. In writing to the seven churches, John conveyed multiple warnings and exhortations to each.

To the church in Ephesus, John affirmed that God was pleased with its works, the members' labor, and their patience "and how you cannot bear with those who are evil, but have tested those who call themselves apostles and are not, and found them to be false. I know you are enduring patiently and bearing up for my name's sake, and you have not grown weary" (Revelation 2:2–3, ESV). However, in spite of their perseverance through conflict, they had lost their first love for Christ. The church's passion for God, and perseverance through conflict, cannot yield to cold, mechanical ritualism.

The church in Smyrna encountered much persecution, but God encouraged it to remain faithful and to not fear as they experienced conflict. As God stated:

> "I know your tribulation and your poverty (but you are rich) and the slander of those who say that they are Jews and are not, but are a synagogue of Satan. Do not fear what you are about to suffer. Behold, the devil is about to throw some of you into prison, that you may be tested, and for ten days you will have tribulation. Be faithful unto death, and I will give you the crown of life. (Revelation 2:8–10, ESV)

While the church in Pergamos compromised its commitment to Christ in various ways, God commended it for not denying the Christian faith even when fellow believers were martyred. God said, "'I know where you dwell, where Satan's throne is. Yet you hold fast my name, and you did not deny my faith even in the days of Antipas my faithful witness, who was killed among you, where Satan dwells" (Revelation 2:13, ESV).

The church of Thyatira was a corrupt church. It permitted sexual immorality to go unchecked. Therefore, because of the church's failure to confront the woman referred to as "Jezebel," and her unwillingness to repent, God promised conflict. It would take the form of sickness, tribulation, and death. God explained, "I will cast her into a sickbed, and those who commit adultery with her into great tribulation, unless they repent of their deeds. I will kill her children with death, and all the churches shall know that I am He who searches the minds and hearts" (Revelation 2.22–23, ESV).

However, to the faithful believers in the church God promised that He would place no additional burden on them and commanded them to "hold fast what you have until I come. The one who conquers and who keeps my works until the end, to him I will give authority over the nations" (Revelation 2:24–26, ESV).

The church at Sardis was rebuked by God as a dead church. There was little commendation given but rather an exhortation to wake up. Such was not the case with the church in Philadelphia.

God encouraged the church in Philadelphia, which had little strength but "have kept My word, and not denied My name" (Revelation 3:8, ESV). God promised the church that "because you have kept my word about patient endurance, I will keep you from the hour of trial that is coming on the whole world, to try those who dwell on the earth" (Revelation 3:10, ESV) He also exhorted them, saying that for those who would persevere through conflict, there would be great reward in heaven (Revelation 3:12, ESV).

Finally, God had no commendation for the church in Laodicea. It was lukewarm in its spiritual commitment to Christ, which made Him sick (Revelation 3:16, ESV). The members were also described as "wretched, pitiable, poor, blind, and naked"

(Revelation 3:17, ESV). The church was not only encouraged to have intimate fellowship with Christ but also to be overcomers in the spiritual walk with Christ (Revelation 3:20–21, ESV). God promised intimate privileges if they were to do so.

John's vivid description concerning worship in heaven both exhorts and instructs leaders who encounter conflict. In Revelation 7, John describes a great multitude of worshipers arrayed in white. They were those who had encountered "great tribulation" and whose robes had been made white in the blood of the Lamb of God, Jesus Christ. The conflicts of earth dissolve in the glories of heaven.

The Scriptures provide ample evidence that God permits, and sometimes directly initiates, conflict in a leader's life for the purpose of developing leadership qualities and abilities that the leader might not otherwise have. What is true in the biblical text holds true today. God continues to use conflict to mold and develop today's godly leaders.

CHAPTER FOUR

Profiles in Conflict: Job's Unwavering Trust in God's Character

> The devil wrestles with God, and the field of battle is the human heart.
>
> —Fyodor Dostoevsky

The book of Job reflects the name of the book's major character. Job's name may mean "the object of hostility" (TWOT, 36), suggesting that he was the object of God's hostility. Another possible meaning is "where is my father" (LaSor, 560). Job's name perhaps refers to his turning to God through the inevitable trials of life. Regardless, Job encountered conflict and suffered for it, while God revealed His own character and purpose in the process.

Job is assumed to have lived during the patriarchal period of biblical history. This is based upon the following factors: (1) Job's age of nearly two hundred years fits the life span of the patriarchal period (42:16, ESV), (2) the patriarchal family structure described in the narrative mirrors this time period, (3) the nomadic Chaldeans who murdered Job's servants and stole his cattle were not yet city dwellers (1:17, ESV), (4) Job's wealth was determined by livestock and not money (1:3 ESV; 42:12, ESV), (5) Job served as his family's priest with no mention of the Levitical priesthood (1:4–5, ESV), and (6) there is no mention of Abraham, Isaac, Jacob, Joseph, or the Mosaic Law. However, Job does refer to Adam (31:33, ESV), the Noahaic Flood (12:15, ESV), and the descendants of Abraham, including the Sabeans (Sheba) who descended from Abraham and Keturah (Genesis 25:1–3 ESV), and Tema, the son of Ishmael (Genesis 25:15 ESV; Isaiah 21:14, ESV).

Job lived in the land of Uz. Uz cannot be precisely located, but it was probably in the Arabian Desert and east of Palestine. This was near the Sabeans and the Chaldeans (Job 1:15–17, ESV). In addition, Job seems to have associated with the people from Mesopotamia, Egypt, and Arabia (6:18–19, ESV; 28:19, ESV; 31:32, ESV).

The Bible describes Job as "blameless and upright, one who feared God and turned away from evil" (Job 1:1, ESV). Job was not sinless (6:24, ESV; 7:21, ESV; 9:20, ESV), but he was a man of character, discipline, integrity, and a godly leader. The text assumes that he was a faithful husband (2:9 ESV) and a godly father with "seven sons and three daughters" (Job 1:1). Taken together, these words describe Job as a man of high moral character.

Job was a wealthy man. He possessed "7,000 sheep, 3,000 camels, 500 yoke of oxen, and 500 female donkeys, and very many servants, so that this man was the greatest of all the people of the east" (Job 1:3, ESV). The Bible further describes him as "the greatest of all the people of the East" (Job 1:3). He was certainly a man of influence.

Job was also a spiritual man. Job regularly offered burnt offerings to God on behalf of his children. The Bible says that "he would rise early in the morning and offer burnt offerings according to the number of them all. For Job said, "It may be that my children have sinned, and cursed God in their hearts." Thus Job did continually (Job 1:5, ESV).

It is in the midst of this background that God and Satan had a conversation. It became a dialogue that would change Job, his family, and his friends. Moreover, the resulting conflict, stemming from God's conversation with Satan and His permission to let him attack the patriarch, would significantly change Job's relationship with the Lord for the better and make him an even greater leader.

The next scene occurred in heaven when the "sons of God came to present themselves before the LORD, and Satan also came among them" (Job 1:6, ESV). After inquiring where Satan had been, as if He needed to, the Lord pointed Job out to the adversary as one who was "a blameless and upright man, who fears God and turns away from evil" (Job 1:8, ESV).

Satan's immediate response called into question Job's faithfulness and commitment to God. He declared that the only reason Job was so righteous was because God had blessed him. Satan declared to God, "but stretch out your hand and touch all that he has, and he will curse you to your face" (Job 1:11, ESV). The Lord gave Satan permission to afflict Job. "Behold, all that he has is in your hand. Only against him do not stretch out your hand" (Job 1:12, ESV). Satan then departed. Job proceeded to lose the following:

- His donkeys and oxen were stolen and the servants were killed by the Sabeans (1:13–15).
- His sheep and servants were destroyed (1:16).
- The Chaldeans raided and stole his camels and killed his servants (1:17).

- Job's children, while eating and drinking in the eldest brother's house, were killed when a great wind struck the house causing it to fall in, killing all who were inside (1:18-19).

Job's response to such tragedy was understandable. He tore his robe and shaved his head and fell to the ground. However, rather than cursing God, as Satan had declared he would, Job worshiped God and said, "Naked I came from my mother's womb, and naked shall I return. The Lord gave, and the Lord has taken away; blessed be the name of the Lord. In all this Job did not sin or charge God with wrong" (Job 1:20–22, ESV).

Satan was still not satisfied. He came to God again. God immediately pointed out that Job remained "a blameless and upright man, who fears God and turns away from evil? He still holds fast his integrity, although you incited me against him to destroy him without reason" (Job 2:3 ESV).

Satan's response was clever; he sought to attack Job's health. "Skin for skin! All that a man has he will give for his life. But stretch out your hand and touch his bone and his flesh, and he will curse you to your face" (Job 2:4–5, ESV). God permitted Satan to attack Job's health with one restriction: "Behold, he is in your hand, but spare his life" (Job 2:6, ESV). Satan proceeded to strike Job "with loathsome sores from the sole of his foot to the crown of his head" (Job 2:7, ESV).

With no knowledge of why this was happening to him, Job took for himself "a piece of broken pottery with which to scrape himself while he sat in the ashes" (Job 2:8, ESV). Job sat on a garbage heap outside the city where he sought to break open the boils, presumably to release the infection. Although the nature of Job's disease is unknown, it was extremely painful.

Job's wife told him to "'curse God and die" (Job 2:9, ESV). However, Job held fast to his integrity and his trust in God. He did not sin with his lips, but He said to her, "You speak as one of the foolish women would speak. Shall we receive good from God, and shall we not receive evil? In all this, Job did not sin with his lips" (Job 2:10, ESV).

Job did not know why he was embroiled into such a conflict. He had no knowledge of the Lord's conversation with Satan. He did not know Satan was testing his integrity. All he knew was that God was trustworthy. In this, he was confident.

This is a significant factor regarding the conflict godly leaders' face: conflict and trials occur only within the parameters of the Lord's sovereign will. Satan is certainly the believer's adversary, but his attack against the Christian is only within the scope of God's providential permission. The devil can only do what God allows.

The Bible affirms that in the midst of spiritual conflict and trials, "no temptation has overtaken you that is not common to man. God is faithful, and he will not let you be tempted beyond your ability, but with the temptation he will also provide the way of escape, that you may be able to endure it" (1 Corinthians 10:13, ESV). Ultimately, whatever the conflict the believer faces, in whatever the form it takes, God is in control. This should provide great comfort for the godly leader in the midst of spiritual conflict.

Shortly after Job's illness, three friends—Eliphaz, Bildad, and Zophar—upon hearing of Job's adversity, came together "to show him sympathy and to comfort him" (Job 2:11, ESV). They were shocked when they saw Job because they did not recognize him. They wept and mourned, and "they sat with him on the ground seven days and seven nights, and no one spoke a word to him, for they saw that his suffering was very great" (Job 2:13, ESV).

However, their initial quietness would eventually give way to a contentious dialogue.

Job's friends were convinced that he had sinned. Otherwise, they reasoned, Job would not be experiencing this profound suffering. They believed conflict and trials were a natural result of disobedience. If not, then they possibly would be susceptible to a similar situation. This began three cycles of discussions and accusations.

In the first cycle, Eliphaz, Bildad, and Zopar respectively counseled Job to repent (4:1–5:27, ESV), to stop impugning God (8:1–22, ESV), and to get right with God (11:1–20, ESV). Following his cry of despair (3:1–16, ESV), Job asked for sympathy (6:1–7:21, ESV), understanding (9:1–10:22, ESV), and he told his friends that they were wrong, all the while hoping that God would speak to him (12:1–14:22, ESV).

In the second cycle, Eliphaz accused Job of presumptuousness (15:1–35, ESV), Bildad declared Job was receiving what he deserved (18:1–21, ESV), and Zophar charged Job with rejecting God by questioning His justice (20:1–29, ESV). Job appealed to God for vindication (16:1–17:16; 19:1–29, ESV) and told Zophar that he was out of touch with reality (21:1–34, ESV).

The third cycle involved only Eliphaz and Bildad, but it retained the same contentious atmosphere. Eliphaz denounced Job's criticism of God's justice (22:1–30), whereas Bildad dismissed Job's appeal to God (25:1–6, ESV). In response, Job declared that God sometimes allows the wicked to prosper in His providential leading (23:1–24:25, ESV), but that God is all wise and sovereign (26:1–14, ESV).

In his final defense, Job maintained his innocence and stated that man cannot discover God's wisdom (27:1–28:28, ESV), and he asked God to defend him (29:1–31:40, ESV). However, it was in this final monologue that Job accused God of being cruel to him and opposing him (30:21–22, ESV). Job maintained his righteousness and elevated it to a place of preeminent pride (30:24–31, ESV). He wanted God to answer him (31:35–37, ESV).

Job's three friends ceased their discussion as did Job. However, a younger man came on the scene: Elihu. His was angry at Job "because he justified himself rather than God" (Job 32:2, ESV).

Elihu charged Job with presumptuousness in criticizing God and not recognizing that God may have had a loving purpose in allowing Job to suffer (33:1–33, ESV). He also declared that Job attacked God's integrity by stating that it did not pay to live a godly life (34:1–37, ESV).

Elihu urged Job to wait on the Lord (35:1–16 ESV) even though he believed God had disciplined Job for some sin (36:1–21, ESV). He concluded by arguing that humans cannot understand God's mercy and justice (36:22–37:24, ESV).

The climatic encounter between God and Job occurred in chapters 38–42 (ESV). Job wanted answers regarding why He was experiencing such conflict. God eventually spoke to Job. However, instead of answering Job, God posed His own series of questions to the beleaguered patriarch.

The final scenes in Job's dramatic story show a humbled patriarch before Almighty God. Yahweh prefaces an extended series of statements in "answering out of the whirlwind" (Job 38:1, ESV) by saying "who is this that darkens counsel by words without knowledge? Dress for action like a man; I will question you, and you make it known to me" (Job 38:2–3, ESV). The Lord demands that Job answer Him regarding the intricacies of creation and the mysteries of life.

God used conflict to teach Job to trust Him. God uses conflict to teach us to trust Him. Bad things do happen to God's people. We face circumstances and situations that seemingly defy explanation. Conflict occurs, often beyond the godly leader's ability to understand why. It is when this happens that one must rely upon the Lord. The godly leader must trust Him in spite of the pain and the unanswered questions. Job's final words to God conveyed this trust:

> I know that You can do everything, and that no purpose of Yours can be withheld from You. You asked, 'Who is this who hides counsel without knowledge?' Therefore I have uttered what I did not understand, things too wonderful for me which I did not know. Listen, please, and let me speak; You said, 'I will question you, and you shall answer Me.' I have heard of You by the hearing of the ear, but now my eyes see you. Therefore I abhor myself, and repent in dust and ashes. (Job 42:2–6, ESV)

When the godly leader experiences the deep pain, suffering, and the conflict of circumstances, he must trust God and His providential leading. As he does, he becomes a leader God uses. What practical principles can we take from Job's conflict?

- Stuff happens!
- Our inability to explain or understand the circumstances happening to us may lead to frustration. How can you overcome such frustration?
- God never promised to answer our questions when difficulties occur. What questions do you presently have for God? If God is not answering your questions, what does He want you to do?
- Why does God want us to trust in Him?

CHAPTER FIVE

Profiles in Conflict: Moses' Endurance by God's Direction

> Now a man of the house of Levi married a Levite woman, and she became pregnant and gave birth to a son.
>
> —Exodus 2:1–2

The Bible makes several statements regarding one of the most significant Old Testament characters: Moses. Perhaps most individual's impressions of Moses are limited to Hollywood movies, and notably actor Charlton Heston, or to a recent feature length cartoon by director/producer Steven Spielberg. While accurate to some extent, these relatively recent interpretations of the "Exodus" fail to fully appreciate the multiple levels of conflict Moses encountered throughout his life.

Studying the biblical text, the student of scripture cannot help but notice the phrases chosen by God to describe Moses' life:

> By faith Moses, when he was grown up, refused to be called the son of Pharaoh's daughter, choosing rather to be mistreated with the people of God than to enjoy the

> fleeting pleasures of sin. He considered the reproach of Christ greater wealth than the treasures of Egypt, for he was looking to the reward. (Hebrews 11:24–26, ESV)

Underlying all these statements, and more, is the constant cloud of conflict. Moses's life was filled with difficulties from birth to death.

When Moses was born, he was hidden for three months by his parents. He was ostensibly abandoned by his parents when he was three months old because Pharaoh issued an order for mass genocide against all male, Hebrew children. He feared the Jews would become so populous they would "multiply, and, if war breaks out, they join our enemies and fight against us and escape from the land" (Exodus 1:10, ESV). It should be noted that this Pharaoh did not know the Hebrew Patriarch Joseph and dealt treacherously with the Jews and oppressed them.

Moses's mother placed him in an ark of bulrushes and "placed it among the reeds by the river bank" (Exodus 2:3, ESV). Pharaoh's daughter found him when she had come to bathe. Moses's mother did not abuse him by setting him adrift. She was desperate. Hebrews 11:23 says that Moses was a "beautiful child." This means "favored" and in this case divinely favored. In this act, we not only see God's providential care, the trust of Moses's mother in the Lord, but also the child's endurance. This would be a characteristic which would be demonstrated numerous times in Moses's life.

Pharaoh's daughter recognized the child as Hebrew. Instead of obeying her father's edict to kill the baby, however, she had compassion upon the child and with no knowledge of her identity directed Moses's sister to find a woman to nurse the child. The maiden found such a woman: Moses's mother. What providential care! There are no coincidences. Eventually, Moses became the son of Pharaoh's daughter. In fact, she gave him the name "Moses" saying, "Because I drew him out of the water" (Exodus 2:10, ESV).

Unaware of the conflict surrounding his birth and his infancy, Moses became the object of God's providential protection and direction. God's perfect plan for Moses and the future nation of Israel would be accomplished not in spite of, but rather because of, the conflict God would ordain. It would not take long for Moses to recognize this conflict initially.

This is true today. God's providential care and guidance continues to help leaders encountering conflict. Conflict is not a punishment from God but rather providential graciousness for the leader to become more like God.

When Moses became of age, he refused to be called the son of Pharaoh's daughter. Moses grew up in the palace of Pharaoh and was reared as the son of Pharaoh's daughter. He benefited greatly in this relationship. Because Moses was a royal prince, he received the best education that the Egyptian palace could provide. In fact, the Bible in Acts 7:22 (ESV) says that "Moses was instructed in all the wisdom of the Egyptians, and he was mighty in his words and deeds."

Yet he cast all this aside when he became of age. How old would Moses have been? The text is not absolutely clear except to imply that Moses had grown up into manhood with its subsequent maturity and responsibilities. In Acts 7:23 (ESV), Stephen indicates Moses was forty years old. Regardless, it was at this time that he made the crucial decision to identify himself no longer with Pharaoh. There was a conflict in his life and his decision underlies this conflict. What was the conflict?

Moses saw that the Egyptians were causing Israel great suffering. Whereas Joseph embraced the position and power of Egypt, Moses turned his back on it all. Why the difference? Under Joseph, Jacob's family found refuge from a devastating famine. In

Moses's day, the famine had given way to prosperity not only for Egypt but especially for the Jews. Due to increasing oppression by Egypt, the time was right for the Hebrews to return to the promised land of Abraham.

In Hebrews 11:25 (ESV), the epistle's writer explains that Moses chose rather to "be mistreated with the people of God than to enjoy the fleeting pleasures of sin." In Acts 7:23 (ESV), Stephen sheds light on the situation when he states that when Moses was "forty years old, it came into his heart to visit his brothers, the children of Israel." Moses witnessed the burdens of his ancestral people. By identifying himself with Israel, Moses turned his back on Egypt. The contrasting choices in his conflict were striking: to suffer affliction with the people of God or enjoy the passing pleasures of sin. He made a choice as to who he was and to whom he would serve.

Why is it important for a leader to take a firm stand when faced with opposition? All conflict involves a battle for truth. While both participants may be wrong in their dispute, they cannot both be right. Therefore, the godly leader must be sure he is right and must not accommodate in his quest and battle for the truth. He must be a student of Scripture and one who applies God's word in all areas of his life.

When a leader accommodates, even a little, he opens the door for further compromise. His leadership becomes questionable. Those he influences will begin to doubt him. He forfeits his integrity. He gains nothing.

The leader must understand that not everyone will like him all the time. Being a leader is not about being liked. It is about leading and influencing people to do what they should do but often ignore or refuse to do. Therefore, the leader must always do what is consistent with God's word. He must study it, know it, apply it, teach it, and live it.

How should a leader take a firm stand in the midst of opposition? Whenever the leader faces controversy, he must demonstrate the following characteristics:

- He must be an instructor. The leader must be a teacher, not only by what he teaches but also by how he consistently lives out what he teaches. In 1 Timothy 4:6 (ESV), the Apostle Paul told his protégé, Timothy, that if he instructed his congregation in the things of God he would be "a good servant of Christ Jesus, being trained in the words of the faith and of the good doctrine that you have followed." The leader must live out what he believes, thereby teaching those he influences how to do the same.
- He must be an exhorter. To exhort means to come along side someone in order to help them. It is easy to reprimand someone whom you disagree with. It is much better to help this individual by patiently encouraging them to understand God's point of view. 1 Timothy 5:1–2 (ESV) says, "Do not rebuke an older man but encourage him as you would a father, younger men as brothers, older women as mothers, younger women as sisters, in all purity."
- He must be humble. Humility means to meekly esteem others better than you. It means to not think arrogantly about your abilities and talents. The leader must be willing to ask himself the tough questions when accused or when involved in conflict.
- He must be an example. This means to be a leader worthy of imitation. How the leader behaves in the midst of opposition will communicate volumes as to his true character. In 1 Timothy 4:12 (ESV) Paul said, "Let no one despise you for your youth, but set the believers an example in speech, in conduct, in love, in faith, in purity." The leader must evaluate

his conduct to see if anything is unbecoming a leader worth following. If there is, he must confess it. If there is not, he must maintain consistency of godly character.

How does the leader sustain his convictions in the midst of opposition?

- He must be biblical. Everything the leader does must be consistent with the word of God. He must plume the depths of God's truth to make sure he is as righteous in behavior as he is in his redeemed position before God. God's word is his standard. He must not deviate from its clear teaching. The leader's commitment to God's truth will give him the authority and courage he needs
- He must have endurance. To endure means to withstand trouble. The leader can only do this by the grace of God, which entails the indwelling presence and power of the Holy Spirit illuminating the word of God into the leader's life. In James 1:2–4 (ESV) says, "Count it all joy, my brothers, when you meet trials of various kinds, for you know that the testing of your faith produces steadfastness. And let steadfastness have its full effect, that you may be perfect and complete, lacking in nothing."

The writer of Hebrews further explains that Moses was a leader who "considered the reproach of Christ greater wealth than the treasures of Egypt, for he was looking to the reward" (Hebrews 11:26, ESV). The retribution he looked forward to was the glory of heaven. In Romans 8:18 (ESV), Paul says, "For I consider that the sufferings of this present time are not worth comparing with the glory that is to be revealed to us." This glorious reward is the resurrection of the body and the perfected righteousness of God in each believer. This was Moses's focus through the conflict he encountered in Egypt. It needs to be our perspective as well.

Moses considered what it meant to forsake Egypt and identify with Israel. What was this prize Moses sought in the midst of such conflict? It was nothing less than the reproach of Christ. Reproach means "defamation" or "disgrace." Moses identified with his peoples suffering by suffering alongside them. Leaders today can identify with the sufferings of the people whom they influence through the sufferings the leader encounters.

The recipients of the Epistle to the Hebrews needed to hear this message. They needed to know that all believers encounter conflict because they identify themselves as God's people and because God uses such conflict to make them stronger believers and effective leaders.

Moses continues to be an example of leadership in the midst of conflict for today's leaders. As God's leaders encounter inevitable conflict, there is the temptation to rest on the side of comfort and accommodation rather than to esteem the reproach of Christ greater than the riches of comfort and compromise. This must not be done. This cannot be done. Whatever peace acquired will be short lived at worst and tenuous at best.

In Hebrews 11:27 (ESV), the writer states, "By faith he left Egypt, not being afraid of the anger of the king, for he endured as seeing him who is invisible." Moses forsook Egypt. The word forsook means "to leave behind" (Strong, 40). It means to abandon. Why did Moses leave Egypt?

The reader must understand that verse 27 is speaking of the time when Moses saw an Egyptian beating a Hebrew and with premeditation killed the Egyptian and hid him in the sand. He soon discovered that the Hebrews knew what he had done. It was then that Moses forsook Egypt because he killed an Egyptian, and he feared Pharaoh's retribution.

Stephen indicated that Moses sought to avenge and defend the Hebrew who was suffering wrong from an Egyptian and that is why he killed him. In Acts 7:25 (ESV), Stephen explains that Moses "supposed that his brothers would understand that God was giving them salvation by his hand, but they did not understand." Moses sought to accomplish God's work his way rather than God's way. This never works.

There have been times when I have been tempted to adopt pragmatic means in order to accomplish God's intended ends. For many in local church ministry, the end, or goal, is to have a large crowd each Sunday. Therefore, using whatever means to achieve that goal seems shrewd or clever. The leader may even believe it to be necessary. Biblically, it is wrong.

The surrounding culture seeks to establish the agenda for the leader. It always has. What the culture accepts is deemed to be right and profitable. However, Scripture indicates that God has established the agenda for life and living. Leadership must submit to God's principles in order to accomplish the work and to live a life glorifying to Him.

After forty years in Midian (Acts 7:30 ESV), God placed Moses into a position of leadership where he would deliver Israel from Egypt's bondage. It would be at the time of the Passover, Exodus 10 (ESV), that Moses was prepared to forsake Egypt a second time, along with Israel, "not being afraid of the anger of the king" (Hebrews 11:27, ESV).

The conflicts of Moses's past prepared him for the responsibilities of the Exodus from Egypt. He endured because he was aware of God. To endure means to be strong and to endure steadily. As one commentator explains, "The only NT instance of εκαρτερησεν [*kartereo*] is in Hebrews 11:27, where Moses, having left Egypt, endured by the faith that reached from He who was invisible but efficacious. This faith in the invisible God is the presupposition of NT faith in the God who has revealed and given himself in Jesus Christ." Moses's loyal leadership of obedience to God was strong; it was as if God had visibly stood before him.

In spite of his conflict with Pharaoh in letting God's people go, Moses demonstrated genuine, biblical, and godly leadership by remaining undeterred in obedience to God. He observed the Passover, along with Israel. By doing so, he and the Jews avoided God's judgment.

This truth had tremendous application to those receiving the Epistle to the Hebrews and to believers today. We should not be afraid of human wrath. Doing what is right, whatever the cost, should be the leader's primary goal. The leader should be gracious in his demeanor, firm in his resolve to address the issue righteously, and enduring through any confrontation. This is not in spite of the conflict but rather because of the conflict.

With this determination to endure, God gives victory. Israel passed though the Red Sea as if on dry ground. The Egyptians who followed drowned. In Acts 7:36, Stephen says, "This man led them out, performing wonders and signs in Egypt and at the Red Sea and in the wilderness for forty years."

How many additional conflicts would occur throughout the forty year wilderness wanderings? In leading Israel, Moses encountered idol worshipers, rebellion, complaining, harlotry, and faithlessness. These are but a few examples, but through each conflict, Moses's leadership remained steadfast.

Moses was not perfect, and any attempt to make him so would bring disservice to the man and the Lord he served. In Numbers 20:1–14 (ESV), Moses's failure to take God at His word at Kadesh resulted in God preventing him from bringing Israel into the Promised Land. Hereto, Moses learned endurance through conflict.

Endurance is not easy. It can be tiring, and often times, the leader is tempted to give up the fight and to give in to the weariness in well doing. This can happen when the leader encounters people who persistently pursue their own agenda rather than the vision and objectives of the company, organization, or the church to which these individuals are a part.

While enduring conflict is not easy, compromise is. The leader may believe, at a weak moment, that it is best to just give in to the pressures surrounding him: to make peace with those who are in opposition. How foolish! For whatever temporary reprieve the leader may derive from concession, it will only placate the sources of conflict temporarily. The next conflict the leader encounters, and there will be a next one, will be tougher to face because of people's probable perception that the leader will always concede rather than confront. What the leader requires is God produced endurance.

God produced endurance in Moses by providing conflict(s) where his faith, tried and tested, overcame adversity. Today, God provides conflict for His children in order for them to learn endurance. Rather than retreat from conflict, leaders ought to embrace and thank God for the conflict and the resulting endurance He develops in them. Through this, an individual becomes the leader God uses.

CHAPTER SIX

Profiles in Conflict: Joseph's Confidence in God's Care

> But as for you, you meant evil against me; but God meant it for good.
>
> —Genesis 50:20

Joseph is one of my heroes. He was one of two men in the Old Testament, Daniel being the second, who did not compromise his relationship with God and fall into scandalous sin. From the moment we meet Joseph as a teenager until his death, he remains faithful to God regardless of the cost. He was a consummate man of integrity and character.

Joseph was just seventeen when his story began (Genesis 37:1–2, ESV). He brought his father Jacob a bad report concerning four of his brothers (the sons of Bilhah and Zilphah) when they were all feeding the flock. Joseph was the son of Rachel (Genesis 35:24, ESV) and was the eleventh of Jacob's twelve sons (Genesis 35:23–26, ESV). He was the grandson of Isaac and the great-grandson of Abraham.

Jacob "loved Joseph more than any other of his sons, because he was the son of his old age" (Genesis 37:3, ESV). Additionally, Jacob made Joseph a "robe of many colors" (Genesis 37:3b, ESV). However the garment appeared, it was a visual reminder to Joseph's brothers that Jacob loved him more. Consequently, they hated Joseph and could not even speak peaceably to him.

In Genesis 37:5–11 (ESV), Joseph's relationship with his brothers further deteriorated when he had two dreams. The first dream involved Joseph and his brothers' binding sheaves in the field. Joseph's sheaf rose and stood upright while his brother's sheaves bowed down to his. The second dream involved the sun, moon, and the eleven stars bowing down to him. The metaphor was that the sun was Jacob, the moon was Rachel, and the eleven stars were his brothers. Upon hearing these two interpretations, the brothers hated Joseph even more and envied him. A brewing conflict was coming to a boil.

Soon after, Joseph's brothers went to feed their father's flock in Shechem. Jacob instructed Joseph to "Go now, see if it is well with your brothers and with the flock, and bring me word. So he sent him from the Valley of Hebron, and he came to Shechem" (Genesis 37:14, ESV). Joseph eventually found his brothers in Dothan.

When Joseph's brothers saw him coming, they conspired to kill him. They said to one another, "Here comes this dreamer. Come now, let us kill him and throw him into one of the pits. Then we will say that a fierce animal has devoured him, and we will see what will become of his dreams" (Genesis 37:18–20, ESV).

The eldest brother, Reuben, disagreed and would not let the others kill Joseph. He sought to deliver Joseph from his brothers and bring him back to Jacob. At Reuben's instructions, the brothers "stripped him of his robe, the robe of many colors that he wore. And they took him and threw him into a pit. The pit was empty; there was no water in it" (Genesis 37:23–24, ESV).

However, before Reuben could deliver Joseph from the pit, the remaining brothers, upon seeing Ishmaelites on their way to Egypt, sold Joseph to the traders for twenty shekels of silver. Apparently, Reuben left his brothers and knew nothing of their further actions. When he returns and finds Joseph gone, his true feelings for his brother and father become evident. He tears his garment as a visible display of grief. The brother's ensuing cover-up involved killing a kid of the goats, dipping Joseph's tunic in the animal's blood and convincing Jacob that Joseph was dead.

In Genesis 37:33–35 (ESV), Jacob was filled with inconsolable grief upon hearing the news that Joseph, supposedly, had been killed. Try as they might, the sons and daughters could not console their father. Jacob "refused to be comforted."

Meanwhile, upon arriving in Egypt the Ishmaelites/Midianites sold Joseph "to Potiphar, an officer of Pharaoh, the captain of the guard" (Genesis 37:36, ESV). Joseph was now a slave in a foreign country. This was just the beginning of his conflicts.

As Joseph began living as Potiphar's slave the Scriptures make it clear that "the LORD was with Joseph, and he became a successful man, and he was in the house of his Egyptian master" (Genesis 39:2, ESV). In addition, Potiphar saw that the Lord was with him and that the Lord brought prosperity onto all which Joseph did.

Joseph grew in responsibility and respect while serving Potiphar. In fact, the Egyptian began to grow fond of Joseph. Potiphar "made him overseer in his house and over all that he had, the LORD blessed the Egyptian's house for Joseph's sake; the blessing of the LORD was on all that he had, in house and field. So he left all that he had in Joseph's charge, and because of him he had no concern about anything but the food he ate" (Genesis

39:5–6, ESV). Potiphar's kindness to Joseph resulted in prosperity for the Egyptian because from the time he had made him overseer of his house the Lord blessed the house because of Joseph.

Joseph was now second man in charge of Potiphar's house. He rose from a pit of betrayal and served in one of the finest homes in Egypt. In fact, Potiphar trusted Joseph so much that he left all that he had in Joseph's hand, and he did not know what he had except for the bread that he ate. Thus far, it seems that the conflict Joseph encountered with his brothers back in Israel paled in comparison to the blessings hc enjoyed in Egypt. The Lord corrected the injustice and Joseph grew in influence. He became a leader in Egypt by being a servant to Potiphar. He experienced the blessings from God and prospered. However, God's process of producing godly leadership qualities in Joseph by conflict was far from complete.

Often, the Bible contains statements that are easily overlooked. They seem, at least to the casual observer, to be insignificant. Yet these statements, wherever they are found in the Scriptures, prove to be precursory to future events. When the Bible says, almost as an aside, that "Joseph was handsome in form and appearance" (Genesis 39:6, ESV) the student of Scripture should take note. There is a reason the narrative contains this sentence. Something is about to happen, and it involves Joseph's attractive appearance.

"And after a time his master's wife cast her eyes on Joseph and said, "Lie with me" (Genesis 39:7, ESV). God tested Joseph? Would Joseph acquiesce to Potiphar's wife's invitation? The Bible says that Joseph refused her advances and said to her:

> Behold, because of me my master has no concern about anything in the house, and he has put everything that he has in my charge. He is not greater in this house than I am, nor has he kept back anything from me except you,

> because you are his wife. How then can I do this great wickedness and sin against God. (Genesis 39:8–9, ESV)

Joseph encountered an intense conflict which has destroyed many a leader: adultery. Yet Joseph stayed noble and true to the holy God he loved and the human master he served. He would not commit what he called, "this great wickedness and sin against God" (Genesis 39:9, ESV).

As it is so often the case with conflict, the temptation continued. Potiphar's wife was relentless. She would not give up. The Bible says "she spoke to Joseph day after day" (Genesis 39:10, ESV). What she said to Joseph is intimated in the statement "that he would not listen to her, to lie beside her or to be with her" (Genesis 39:10, ESV). Joseph remained true to God in spite of intense conflict. He would not compromise his convictions, but neither would Potiphar's wife alter her desires.

Desperate people often do desperate things. Or as filmmaker and comedian Woody Allen stated in explaining his sexual affair with his wife's adopted daughter, "The heart wants what it wants… There's no logic to those things" (Twilight, par. 26). Potiphar's wife wanted Joseph and was willing to go to great lengths to entrap him. "But one day, when he went into the house to do his work and none of the men of the house was there in the house, she caught him by his garment, saying, "Lay with me." But he left his garment in her hand and fled and got out of the house" (Genesis 39:11–12, ESV).

Potiphar's wife set the trap. Joseph refused to take the bait. He did what every leader should do in a similar situation but often do not: he ran away. He did not debate, nor did he try to reason with Potiphar's wife. He ran away from her. He got as far away from her as he could. Joseph did the right thing. But wait! The woman was not done.

"Heaven has no rage like love to hatred turned, nor hell a fury like a woman scorned" (Bartlett, par. 1). It did not take long for Potiphar's wife to turn against Joseph. She wanted him, but he refused. Therefore, she became determined to destroy him any way she could.

She called to the men of the house and falsely accused Joseph of attempted rape. She then told Potiphar the same story. His reaction was normal; he became angry. Potiphar put Joseph into prison. There was no trial or any opportunity for Joseph to defend himself but rather a quick confinement for something he did not do. The irony is that Joseph was confined even though he did the right thing by running away. How do we make sense of this?

The Scriptures do not attempt to explain to Joseph or to leaders today, the reason God permitted these events to occur. The Bible says only that "the Lord was with Joseph and showed him steadfast love and gave him favor in the sight of the keeper of the prison" (Genesis 39:21, ESV). The Scriptures further state that:

> And the keeper of the prison put Joseph in charge of all the prisoners who were in the prison. Whatever was done there, he was the one who did it. The keeper of the prison paid no attention to anything that was in Joseph's charge, because the Lord was with him. And whatever he did, the Lord made it succeed. (Genesis 39:22–23, ESV)

God did not forsake Joseph in the midst of conflict, and He does not forsake His children today. This includes godly leaders who are currently in the midst of conflict. He has a purpose and a plan for each leader and uses conflict for a greater purpose than one's immediate comfort and prosperity.

What was God's purpose for Joseph's life? At this particular time, Joseph had no way of knowing that God would use prison to prepare him for even greater responsibilities. At this point in his life, all Joseph could do was trust God. God was all he had. God was all he needed.

After an undetermined period of time, Pharaoh imprisoned two of his servants who had offended and angered him: the butler and the baker. The text does not say how they angered Pharaoh or what prompted the king to imprison them. However, they were placed in the area where Joseph was confined. The captain of the guard "appointed Joseph to be with them, and he attended them. They continued for some time in custody" (Genesis 40:4, ESV).

Soon thereafter, both the butler and the baker had a dream. Each dream was different, and each one had its own meaning. The next morning, Joseph saw that both men were sad. He asked them both what was wrong, and the men replied that each had a dream, but there was no one to interpret their dreams. Joseph indicated that he could and that he would interpret the dreams. Both men proceeded to relate their particular stories to him.

The butler dreamt that a vine was before him and "on the vine there were three branches. As soon as it budded, its blossoms shot forth, and the clusters ripened into grapes" (Genesis 40:9–10, ESV). Then the butler had Pharaoh's cup in his hand, and he pressed the grapes into the cup and gave the cup to Pharaoh.

Joseph interpreted that the three branches were three days and that within that period of time, Pharaoh would restore the butler to his place of responsibility. Upon completing the interpretation for the butler, Joseph asked that he remember him when "it is well with you, and please do me the kindness to mention me to Pharaoh, and so get me out of this house" (Genesis 40:14, ESV). Joseph proclaimed his innocence to the butler. He also said that not only was he stolen from his home, but also he had done nothing to warrant being in prison.

Joseph then interpreted the baker's dream. The baker dreamt there were three white baskets on his head and in the uppermost basket were all kinds of baked goods for Pharaoh. However, birds ate them out of the basket. The baker was quite excited upon hearing the favorable interpretation of the butler's dream, but unfortunately, his outcome would be different. Joseph stated the baskets also represented three days, but that within that period of time, Pharaoh would execute the baker and the birds would pick at his flesh.

Joseph's interpretations came true. Pharaoh reinstated the butler but hanged the baker. However, the butler failed to tell Pharaoh about Joseph. "Yet the chief cupbearer did not remember Joseph, but forgot him" (Genesis 40:23, ESV). Joseph would reside in prison two more years before God would choose to use him in an even greater area of influence developed through the conflict Joseph already encountered. The Scriptures record:

> After two whole years, Pharaoh dreamed that he was standing by the Nile, and behold, there came up out of the Nile seven cows attractive and plump, and they fed in the reed grass. And behold, seven other cows, ugly and thin, came up out of the Nile after them, and stood by the other cows on the bank of the Nile. And the ugly, thin cows ate up the seven attractive, plump cows. And Pharaoh awoke. (Genesis 41:1–4, ESV)

As if this dream was not disturbing enough, Pharaoh had a second dream:

> And he fell asleep and dreamed a second time. And behold, seven ears of grain, plump and good, were growing on one stalk. And behold, after them sprouted seven ears, thin and

> blighted by the east wind. And the thin ears swallowed up the seven plump, full ears. And Pharaoh awoke, and behold, it was a dream. (Genesis 41:5–7, ESV)

Pharaoh was troubled as a result of these dreams. "So in the morning his spirit was troubled, and he sent and called for all the magicians of Egypt and all its wise men. Pharaoh told them his dreams, but there was none who could interpret them to Pharaoh" (Genesis 41:8, ESV). Anyone that is except Joseph.

The chief butler, whom Joseph encountered in prison, came to Pharaoh and told him he knew a prisoner who correctly interpreted dreams. Upon hearing this, Pharaoh sent for Joseph.

When Joseph came to Pharaoh, the king of Egypt stated, "I have had a dream, and there is no one who can interpret it. I have heard it said of you that when you hear a dream you can interpret it" (Genesis 41:15, ESV). Joseph's reply revealed his integrity and his leadership. "It is not in me; God will give Pharaoh a favorable answer" (Genesis 41:16, ESV). Joseph acknowledged God's work in his life. He claimed no personal glory for himself but rightly directed it to God.

Pharaoh proceeded to explain his two dreams to Joseph. Joseph's answer from the Lord was immediately forthcoming. Joseph told Pharaoh that both dreams had the same meaning and that "the thing is fixed by God, and God will shortly bring it about" (Genesis 41:32, ESV).

Joseph explained to the king that the seven good cows, and the seven good heads of grain, both represented seven years. They symbolized seven years of abundance throughout all the land of Egypt. However, the seven thin and ugly cows, along with seven empty heads of grain, represented seven years of famine and these years of famine would wipe out the seven years of abundance. Joseph indicated to Pharaoh that the dream was repeated in order to show the king that God will shortly bring it to pass. What was Pharaoh, and Egypt, to do? Joseph, in the midst of an impending conflict which would affect the entire region, did not waste much time in giving Pharaoh counsel. He stated:

> Now therefore let Pharaoh select a discerning and wise man, and set him over the land of Egypt. Let Pharaoh proceed to appoint overseers over the land and take one-fifth of the produce of the land of Egypt during the seven plentiful years. And let them gather all the food of these good years that are coming and store up grain under the authority of Pharaoh for food in the cities, and let them keep it. That food shall be a reserve for the land against the seven years of famine that are to occur in the land of Egypt, so that the land may not perish through the famine. (Genesis 41:33–36, ESV)

Joseph knew first hand God's supernatural care during times of conflict. Having been sold into slavery by his brothers, falsely accused by Potiphar's wife, and unjustly imprisoned and forgotten, Joseph could have become a bitter man. However, he became a godly leader that God chose to use to save a nation from starvation.

Conflict can lead to feelings of loneliness, despair, and bitterness when the leader focuses upon the circumstances rather than the Lord. Joseph could easily have done this in light of the treachery he experienced. It is most important for the leader to not only know that God is in control of life's circumstances but also to resolve to be obedient in the midst of those circumstances by trusting in the Lord.

The leader's trust that God is in control is strengthened by consistent reading and meditation in God's word: the Bible.

Filling your mind with God's truth brings comfort that you are not alone. As He was with Joseph, so He is with you.

Coupled with this is the discipline of heartfelt prayer to God. When the leader pours out his fears and anxiety to God, the result is a calming peace. I have witnessed this in the hospital room with a dying man surrounded by family and in the living room of a person facing the issue of a prodigal child. Calling out to God acknowledges a greater authority than our own.

The leader should also associate with a few, select, spiritually mature friends. These individuals encourage, listen, and when necessary, tell the leader what he needs to hear rather than what he wants to hear. These are the people the leader can count on for honest evaluation. These are his staunch supporters. They are to be cherished.

Pharaoh thought Joseph's advice was good and recognized the Spirit of God was with him. Therefore, Pharaoh appointed Joseph over all the people of Egypt, second only to Pharaoh in authority. Pharaoh gave Joseph a signet ring, clothed him in fine linen garments, and put a gold chain around his neck. Pharaoh gave Joseph an Egyptian name, Zaphnath-Paaneah, and also gave him a wife, Asenath, who was the daughter of an Egyptian priest.

Joseph was now thirty years of age. Thirteen years of conflict, betrayal, slavery, and imprisonment resulted in him becoming the second most powerful man in Egypt. God used conflicts and trials to mold and shape Joseph to become the godly leader Egypt needed. Joseph was vindicated. Egypt was spared. The remaining issue in Joseph's leadership journey was for him to reconcile with his family, specifically his brothers. The time for reconciliation was at hand.

The seven-year famine arrived, and it was so severe that it affected all the lands neighboring Egypt. Genesis 41:56 (ESV) indicates that "when the famine had spread over all the land,

Joseph opened all the storehouses and sold to the Egyptians, for the famine was severe in the land of Egypt." Additionally, all countries came to Joseph in Egypt to buy grain because the famine was very severe.

When Jacob realized there was grain in Egypt, he ordered his ten eldest sons to go down to Egypt. He said, "Behold, I have heard that there is grain for sale in Egypt. Go down and buy grain for us there, that we may live and not die" (Genesis 42:2, ESV).

So Joseph's ten brothers went down to buy grain in Egypt. But Jacob did not send Joseph's brother Benjamin with his brothers, for he "feared that harm might happen to him" (Genesis 42:4, ESV). And the sons of Israel went to buy grain among those who journeyed, for the famine was in the land of Canaan.

God set the stage for Joseph's eventual reunion with his brothers and his father. Joseph's journey as a leader involved him confronting his brothers who wronged him.

You have probably thought about what you would do as a leader if you had the opportunity to confront the source of your conflict. Perhaps you have rehearsed the words you would say, practiced the tone of your voice for that moment, and imagined the eventual outcome of reckoning.

When Joseph's brothers arrived in Egypt, they came to Joseph and "bowed down before him with their faces to the earth" (Genesis 42:6, ESV). Joseph recognized his brothers, but they did not recognize him. He accused them of being spies, a charge the brothers adamantly denied. They did not realize that Joseph was alive and before them.

Joseph wanted to see if his brothers were men of integrity. While imprisoning his brothers for three days, he devised a plan to test his brothers. He explained to them that if they were honest men, they would agree to let one of their brothers be confined to the prison house while the rest would go and carry grain back home. Then they were to return to Egypt with their youngest brother, Benjamin, with them.

The brothers agreed to Joseph's terms because they had no choice. They discussed among themselves their guilt for having sold Joseph into slavery thirteen years earlier and that this was the reason for their troubles. They recalled their brother's pleadings and the anguish of his soul. Reuben explained that Joseph's "blood is now required of us." All the while, Joseph understood what they were saying. Joseph imprisoned Simeon while the others journeyed back to Canaan.

What would the brothers do? Would they allow Simeon to rot in jail? Would Joseph kill Simeon if the brothers did not return with Benjamin? Would Jacob allow Benjamin to journey to Egypt in order to save Simeon? What would Joseph do if Benjamin did arrive in Egypt? These critical questions arise from the fires of conflict, sparked by Joseph's brother's actions thirteen years earlier. The answers to these questions would reflect the leader Joseph was, and the leaders his brothers would become.

As a leader facing conflict, there is a tendency to view difficulties solely from our perspective. We may be quick to see injustices done by other people toward us, but we rarely examine what we have done to others. The leader of integrity examines his heart to see what wickedness to confess. He is honest with himself, which is not always easy.

Following this, a leader must examine how he will treat those who wronged him. Will he extract his revenge or demonstrate grace? Will he entrust his life and circumstances to God's providential care? The leader of integrity must submit to God's sovereign control in life's circumstances. He must not allow bitterness and resentment for past wrongs to hinder him from doing what is right.

The brothers returned to Canaan with sacks filled with grain along with provisions for the journey. Joseph also restored to each one, without their knowledge, their money they spent for the grain. Upon discovering the money in their sacks, they were confused and afraid and exclaimed, "What is this that God has done to us?"

Rather than obtaining revenge, the leader displays benevolent grace. He embodies what the apostle Paul stated in Ephesians 4:31–32 (ESV), "Let all bitterness and wrath and anger and clamor and slander be put away from you, along with all malice. Be kind to one another, tenderhearted, forgiving one another, as God in Christ forgave you." The leader understands the grace he gives can never equal the grace God has given.

Upon arriving back home, the brothers told Jacob all that happened in Egypt and on the return trip. Jacob responded in self-pity. "You have bereaved me of my children: Joseph is no more, and Simeon is no more, and now you would take Benjamin. All this has come against me" (Genesis 42:36, ESV).

An unspecified time period elapsed, and the famine remained severe (Genesis 43:1, ESV). Having exhausted the grain purchased in Egypt, Jacob instructed his sons to return to Egypt and "buy us a little food." However, Judah told his father that they could not return to Egypt without Benjamin.

Reuben made a salutary appeal to Jacob by saying, "Kill my two sons if I do not bring him back to you. Put him in my hands, and I will bring him back to you" (Genesis 42:37, ESV). Jacob would have none of it. He would not allow Benjamin to accompany the brothers back to Egypt. He could not stand the thought that something would happen to Benjamin. Ironically, Jacob seems completely resigned to Simeon's death, even though he is not certain of his son's fate.

While conflict brought out the best in Joseph, it brought out the worst in Jacob. He complained and thought only of himself while the world was in the midst of great suffering. Pressure sometimes does this to people. The rest of the world may be falling apart, but certain people focus only on their problems. They react with self-centeredness and speak foolishly.

Jacob shows us what not to do when facing conflict. He concentrated upon his circumstances and not upon the sovereign God who works through the circumstances of life. Jacob knew better. He had witnessed God's work in his young life. However, the lessons of youth were somehow lost in his old age.

Lest we judge Jacob too harshly, it would do well for us to examine where our attention is when our conflicts reach their apex. Do we recognize God's sovereign working through our circumstances, or are we overwhelmed by them? Do we acknowledge the truth of 2 Timothy 3:12 (ESV) where it says, "Indeed, all who desire to live a godly life in Christ Jesus will be persecuted." As leaders, we either follow the master of our circumstances or we become mastered by our circumstances. It is a truth we must remember.

Finally, Judah assumed responsibility and pledged to protect Benjamin at all costs. Jacob reluctantly agreed and instructed his sons as to what presents to bring to whom he called "the man," not knowing it was his own son. He stated, "May God Almighty grant you mercy before the man, and may he send back your other brother and Benjamin. And as for me, if I am bereaved of my children, I am bereaved" (Genesis 43:14, ESV). The brothers, including Benjamin, traveled back to Egypt.

Upon their arrival, all eleven brothers stood before Joseph. As Joseph provided for their needs, the brothers admitted to Joseph's steward about their money for the grain they purchased being in their sacks following their first journey and their desire to render payment, not only for their present needs but also for what Joseph had given them. The brothers displayed a genuine attitude of confession and repentance. The steward told them not to worry, and then, he brought Simeon to them.

The brothers' display appeared to be genuine. God's life lessons were taking effect. They were becoming men of integrity, not only toward their father and youngest brother but also toward Joseph.

After exchanging pleasantries, inquiring about his father Jacob, and seeing his brother Benjamin for the first time in thirteen years, Joseph was overcome with emotion. He arranged a dinner for all of them, seating each brother according to his age. The brothers were astonished at this peculiarity. In addition, Joseph served Benjamin with five times more food than the rest. It was a merry time, but a precursor to the ultimate test Joseph would conduct with his brothers to see if they truly had changed.

Joseph had a plan. He directed that each of his brother's sacks be filled with as much food as they could carry. Additionally, Joseph instructed his steward to place a silver cup in the sack of Benjamin. The next morning, the brothers began their journey back home, not knowing the silver cup was in their youngest brother's sack.

According to his scheme, Joseph immediately sent his steward to overtake his brother's and say, "Why have you repaid evil for good? Is it not from this that my lord drinks, and by this that he practices divination? You have done evil in doing this" (Genesis 44:4–5, ESV). Joseph set his brothers up to see if they would forsake Benjamin in order to save their own lives. Would this conflict reveal their integrity or rather their willingness to sacrifice another for their own well being?

When they were accused, the brothers denied they had stolen anything from the man who was their brother. They were so confident of this that they even stated that "whichever of your servants is found with it shall die, and we also will be my lord's servants." He said, "Let it be as you say: he who is found with it shall be my servant, and the rest of you shall be innocent" (Genesis 44:9–10, ESV). To their horror, the cup was found in Benjamin's sack. The brothers tore their clothes in anguish and proceeded back to Egypt. What would they do, or say, when their brother, whom they only knew as an Egyptian, confronted them?

Upon reaching Joseph's house, Judah spoke for them all when he said, "What shall we say to my lord? What shall we speak? Or how can we clear ourselves? God has found out the guilt of your servants; behold, we are my lord's servants, both we and he also in whose hand the cup has been found" (Genesis 44:16, ESV). Judah, and his brothers, claimed equal responsibility for Benjamin's presumed transgression. Would this be enough to satisfy Joseph that his brothers indeed had changed from what they were thirteen years earlier?

Joseph provided one final provision to test his older brother's character and in response to Judah's statement that all the brothers would serve as Joseph's slaves. Whoever possesses the cup would become Joseph slave while the rest could return home.

This was the ultimate test. The conflict was joined. The brothers would make a decision. They could travel back to Canaan and fabricate some story for Jacob about Benjamin's enslavement, all the while enjoying a relatively, comfortable life. Or they could be men of character and leadership, as Joseph was, and intercede on their brother's behalf. Judah made the decision.

Judah interceded upon Benjamin's behalf. He was eloquent and passionate. He spoke of Jacob and his love for Benjamin. He spoke of the circumstances leading up to the eleven brothers coming to Egypt a second time. He related that Jacob would die if Benjamin did not return home. He shared that he (Judah) would personally bear the blame (Genesis 44:18–32, ESV).

Finally, Judah made the ultimate statement of love, character, and leadership. Not thinking of himself but of Benjamin and Jacob, Judah said, "Now therefore, please let your servant remain instead of the boy as a servant to my lord, and let the boy go back with his brothers. For how can I go back to my father if the boy is not with me? I fear to see the evil that would find my father" (Genesis 44:33–34, ESV). The grace Judah expressed toward Benjamin was what he had failed to give Joseph years ago. Judah had changed. The brothers had changed. They were no longer the same men.

The cycle was complete. Joseph's brothers became men of character and leadership by the crucible of conflict, as had Joseph. Through the conflict of Simeon's imprisonment and Joseph's proposed enslavement of Benjamin, the elder brothers developed character in refusing to let this happen, especially Judah. It was not until Joseph knew for sure what their true intentions were that he finally revealed himself to his brothers.

The disharmony and difficulty that had existed for so long in Jacob's family gave way to reconciliation and reunion. Joseph and his brothers became closer to each other than they had ever been. Jacob was reunited with a son long thought dead, and Egypt, and its surrounding civilizations, was saved from starvation.

Joseph's legacy could best be summarized by his own words when he said to his brothers, "As for you, you meant evil against me, but God meant it for good, to bring it about that many people should be kept alive, as they are today" (Genesis 50:20, ESV). Joseph's statement is the classic answer regarding God's sovereignty over man's affairs.

However, the student of Scripture must recognize that God sovereignly directed Joseph through some of the most difficult circumstances imaginable to bring him to the eventuality of what he spoke. Joseph's words were not trite and clichéd, but they represented an honest and correct reflection of Biblical truth, truth which God continues to communicate to His children that He is trustworthy. A godly leader can have confidence in God's care.

While we may never experience the same conflicts Joseph and his brothers encountered, God will certainly use whatever difficulties we face to develop us into leaders glorifying to Him. Joseph's integrity of character was evident throughout his life's experiences, while his brother's integrity had to be developed. Regardless, godly character is the primary goal for God bringing conflicts into our lives. Ask yourself the following questions regarding your current conflicts.

- What conflict(s) are you now experiencing?
- Who can you identify as the secondary source of your conflict, with God being the primary source? How have you contributed to the conflict?
- Thus far, how have you been effected by the conflict? Are you bitter? Angry? Impatient? Humbled? Sad? Joyful?
- What areas of character development do you see God accomplishing in you?
- What do others see God accomplishing in your life.

CHAPTER SEVEN

Profiles in Conflict: David's Heartfelt Commitment to Uphold God's Glory!

For the Lord does not see as man sees; for man looks at the outward appearance, but the Lord looks at the heart.

—1 Samuel 16:7b

How often does the public evaluate successful leaders by outward circumstances rather than inner character? More often than not, the world's prevailing perspective concerning leaders is that image is everything. If things are looking good and the leader gives forth an appearance of success, then everything must be okay. Even if things are not as they ought to be, the so-called leader has a slew of public relations people who will put a positive spin on every situation.

For many, character has become a commodity. It is viewed today as an article of trade. The only remaining question is, at what cost? Magazines, newspapers, movies, and television emphasize the most beautiful, the best, and the brightest. Talent, ability, and integrity give way to money, success, and celebrity. However, character is a mile wide and an inch deep.

One wonders how the chief executive and chief financial officers of Enron, Tyco, and WorldCom are now viewed by the public in the wake of scandals, bankruptcy, and prison sentencing. Kenneth Lay, Dennis Kozlowski, Mark Swartz, and Bernard Ebbers respectively were to many the poster children of greed and avarice.

Additionally, major league baseball took a public relations hit during the 2005 season with the revelation by, and subsequent punishment of, several players discovered to have taken steroids or performance-enhancing drugs. The Baltimore Orioles Rafael Palmiero told the United States Congress, under oath, that he never took steroids, yet it was later discovered he had indeed taken a banned substance. What consequences await him has yet to be determined. Has the so-called national pastime been tainted beyond repair? Even the New York Yankees Alex Rodriguez has confessed to using steroids.

Former President George W. Bush found his popularity falling, according to several pollsters, because of his apparent inaction in responding to the Hurricane Katrina crisis in New Orleans, Louisiana, and the United States military involvement in Iraq. One full-page AD in the *USA Today* branded the president, former Vice-President Chaney, and former Secretary of State Colin Powell as liars. Many people, especially the group known as The People for the American Way, perceived these men as leaders who lacked character.

Several years ago, Promise Keepers hosted a pastor's conference in Indianapolis, Indiana. One of the keynote speakers was noted author and pastor Chuck Swindoll. The title of his message was *The Heart of a Great Leader*, and his text was Proverbs 4:20–27 (ESV):

> My son, be attentive to my words; incline your ear to my sayings. Let them not escape from your sight; keep them within your heart. For they are life to those who find them, and healing to all their flesh. Keep your heart with all vigilance, for from it flow the springs of life. Put away from you crooked speech, and put devious talk far from you. Let your eyes look directly forward, and your gaze be straight before you. Ponder the path of your feet; then all your ways will be sure. Do not swerve to the right or to the left; turn your foot away from evil.

Pastor Swindoll told those assembled that the most important component of their lives as leaders was their heart and that it takes great heart to be a great leader. Throughout this book, the overriding theme has been God's impact upon a godly leader's heart through conflict.

The Old Testament Hebrew word for heart is "בָּבֵל." (*qamay*), and it refers to a human's "feelings, intellect, and the most interior center of an individual. It may also refer to courage and understanding."

> Concrete meanings of בָּבֵל referred to the internal organ and to analogous physical locations. However, in its abstract meanings, "heart" became the richest biblical term for the totality of man's inner or immaterial nature. In biblical literature it is the most frequently used term for man's immaterial personality functions as well as the most inclusive term for them since, in the Bible, virtually every immaterial function of man is attributed to the "heart". In many contexts, it expresses the totality of a man's nature and character, both inner and outer. (*Theological Workbook of the Old Testament*)

The Greek words for heart are "καρδια" (*kardia*) and "ψυχης" (*psuche*). While καρδια may refer to the chief organ of physical life, both καρδια and ψυχης describe the inner being of man including "feelings, desires and passions." W. E. Vine explains that καρδια "came to stand for man's entire mental and moral activity, both rational and the emotional elements." Gerard Kittel states that ψυχης speaks of the "soul or life."

Proverbs 4 indicates that godly leaders must guard their hearts above all else. They do so by guarding what they say, what they watch, where they go, and what they do. Why? Honestly, it is because "out of the heart of man, come evil thoughts, sexual immorality, theft, murder, adultery, coveting, wickedness, deceit, sensuality, envy, slander, pride, foolishness. All these evil things come from within, and they defile a person" (Mark 7:21–23, ESV).

The Bible instructs believers that leaders should believe God with all their heart (Acts 8:37, ESV; Romans 10:10, ESV), serve God with all their heart (Deuteronomy 11:13, ESV), and keep His statutes with all their heart (Deuteronomy 26:16, ESV). In addition, godly leaders are to trust in God with all their heart (Proverbs 3:5–6, ESV), love God with all their heart (Matthew 22:37, ESV), and do the will of God from the heart (Ephesians 6:6, ESV). Believers are also to sanctify God in their hearts (1 Peter 3:15, ESV), and love one another with a pure heart (1 Peter 1:22, ESV).

Therefore, it is not surprising that the Lord, in 1 Samuel 13 (ESV), commanded Samuel not to look upon the physical appearance of a man as a qualification to be the King of Israel but rather to look on the heart. King Saul, Israel's first king, disqualified himself from holding the position because of his disobedience and unlawful sacrifice. In 1 Samuel 13:13–14 (ESV), Samuel told Saul following the incident:

> You have done foolishly. You have not kept the command of the Lord your God, with which he commanded you. For then the Lord would have established your kingdom over Israel forever. But now your kingdom shall not continue. The Lord has sought out a man after his own heart, and the Lord has commanded him to be prince over his people, because you have not kept what the Lord commanded you.

Who would succeed Saul as king? Samuel left no doubt when he stated, "But now your kingdom shall not continue. The Lord has sought out a man after his own heart, and the Lord has commanded him to be prince over his people, because you have not kept what the Lord commanded you" (1 Samuel 13:14, ESV).

Who would be this man after God's own heart? The Lord told Samuel to go to the home of Jesse, who lived in Bethlehem. God told Samuel that one of Jesse's sons would be Israel's new king. God further told Samuel his reason for selecting one of Jesse's sons in 1 Samuel 16:7 (ESV). "Do not look on his appearance or on the height of his stature, because I have rejected him. For the Lord sees not as man sees: man looks on the outward appearance, but the Lord looks on the heart" (1 Samuel 16:7, ESV). David would be God's choice for king. He was a man after God's own heart, whom Samuel anointed to be King of Israel.

Several authors have written books about David. He is a significant biblical character, inspiring gifted writers to meditate about his integrity, leadership, and devotion to God. Several of these books are best sellers and grace the shelves of pastors and parishioners alike. Therefore, great care must be exhibited in examining David's life. What else can be written that has not already been stated?

David's walk with God consumes a significant volume of the Old Testament, along with many references to him in the New Testament. What specifically should be included and what should be left out in this examination concerning David's leadership?

Let's focus only on two incidents in David's life where he encountered conflict. These were not the only times he faced trials, but these situations are not only well known, but they also show the significance of conflict in developing godly leadership and the terrible price when a godly man falters. The incidents referenced arc David's commitment to uphold God's glory in his battle with Goliath and his moral failure with Bathsheba.

The Bible initially mentions David when he is seemingly a forgotten man, forgotten by his earthly father but not his heavenly Father. The immediate context is found in 1 Samuel 16:1–13 (ESV). The Lord instructed Samuel to fill his horn with oil and go to the home of a resident of Bethlehem named Jesse because God had selected "a king among his sons." God rejected Israel's first king, Saul, because of his rebelliousness and disobedience to God.

Upon his arrival, Samuel invited Jesse and his sons to the sacrifice God instructed the judge to perform using a heifer. Samuel looked at Jesse's son Eliab and concluded that the Lord's anointed was before Him. However, in 1 Samuel 16:7 (ESV), the Lord said, "Do not look on his appearance or on the height of his stature, because I have rejected him. For the LORD sees not as man sees: man looks on the outward appearance, but the LORD looks on the heart."

Jesse made seven of his sons, including Abinadab and Shammah, pass before Samuel to see which one would be the Lord's anointed king over Israel. However, God chose none of them.

Finally, Samuel asked Jesse, "Are all your sons here?" And he said, "There remains yet the youngest, but behold, he is keeping the sheep." And Samuel said to Jesse, "Send and get him, for we will not sit down till he comes here" (1 Samuel 16:11, ESV). As with Isaac, Jacob, and Joseph, God favored the least noticed and the youngest. The shepherd boy would become a mighty king. David would foreshadow the King of kings: Jesus Christ.

Samuel instructed Jesse to bring his youngest son to him. Jesse's youngest son was ruddy, with bright eyes, and good looking. The Lord told Samuel, "Arise, anoint him, for this is he" (1 Samuel 16:12, ESV). Samuel took the horn of oil and anointed him in the midst of his brothers; and the Spirit of the Lord came upon David from that day forward.

God's choosing of David to be Israel's next king had nothing to do with his appearance. God selected David because he was a man whose heart was dedicated to Him. This would soon be seen, not only by King Saul, but also by a Philistine named Goliath.

It was shortly after David's anointing that he began to serve in the palace of King Saul. When the Spirit of the Lord departed from Saul, a distressing spirit from the Lord began to trouble him. Saul's servants implored the king to allow them to find a musician. "Let our lord now command your servants who are before you to seek out a man who is skillful in playing the lyre, and when the harmful spirit from God is upon you, he will play it, and you will be well" (1 Samuel 16:16, ESV). Saul agreed and David was selected. Saul's servants described him as one "who is skillful in playing, a man of valor, a man of war, prudent in speech, and a man of good presence, and the LORD is with him" (1 Samuel 16:18, ESV).

David was a faithful servant to the king. In fact, the Bible says that Saul loved David greatly, and he became his armor-bearer. Whenever the king became distressed, David would take a harp and play it with his hand. Then Saul would become refreshed and well, and the distressing spirit would leave.

Israel's future king is growing in privilege and responsibility. However, he is an anointed king poised to encounter severe conflict.

As 1 Samuel 17 (ESV) unfolds, the armies of Israel and the Philistines were ready to fight against each other. Encamped northwest of Bethlehem, "Saul and the men of Israel were gathered, and encamped in the Valley of Elah, and drew up in line of battle against the Philistines" (1 Samuel 17:2, ESV). With a valley between them, each army stood prepared for battle on a mountain.

However, the Philistines had an advantage: a man named Goliath. Goliath was a champion from the Philistine city called Gath and stood approximately nine feet and nine inches tall. He wore the following hardware: a bronze helmet, a coat of mail weighing 125 pounds, bronze armor on his legs, and a bronze javelin between his shoulders. He also had a spear, which weighed fifteen pounds. He was an intimidating presence. In 1 Samuel 17:8–10 (ESV), Goliath made a proposition to the Israeli army:

> He stood and shouted to the ranks of Israel, "Why have you come out to draw up for battle? Am I not a Philistine, and are you not servants of Saul? Choose a man for yourselves, and let him come down to me. If he is able to fight with me and kill me, then we will be your servants. But if I prevail against him and kill him, then you shall be our servants and serve us." And the Philistine said, "I defy the ranks of Israel this day. Give me a man, that we may fight together."

The reaction from the Israeli army was fear: they were scared. 1 Samuel 17:11 (ESV) says that "When Saul and all Israel heard these words of the Philistine, they were dismayed and greatly afraid." Israel was confused. They did not know what to do and were paralyzed with fear. This included King Saul.

Saul and his army encountered armed conflict before, but there was something about this one man, taunting an entire army, which stopped them in their tracks. What was it? It seems that Israel in general, and King Saul in particular, was more concerned with outward appearances and was also influenced by the fear of men.

It was a nightmare that continued for forty days and nights. For over a month, both morning and evening, Goliath made his proposition to Israel. He continued to taunt and intimidate, and no one took him up on his offer, neither King Saul nor any other seasoned soldier.

Conflict can do this. It can render a normally competent and confident leader incapable of making a decision, confronting a situation, or handling a difficulty. Often, the response is fear, accommodation, or flight in the mistaken notion that inaction will make the conflict just go away. However, this will not happen, then or now. Was there no one who would join the battle and engage the Philistine in combat?

For David, the day he fought Goliath began just like any other day. As the youngest son of Jesse, he would occasionally leave the palace of King Saul and return to feed his father's flocks. Not only that, but he would also run errands for his father; such was the case that fateful day.

Jesse told David to take about a bushel of grain and ten loaves to his older brothers at the camp of the Israeli army. The brothers who went off to war were Jesse's three eldest: Eliab, Abinadab, and Shammah. In addition, David took ten cheeses to the captain of the army thousand. Jesse also wanted to know how David's brothers were doing. David got up early in the morning, left the sheep with a keeper, and took the things and went as Jesse had told him.

David arrived at the army's camp when the army was going out to fight. The Philistines and the Israelis were ready to engage in conflict. David came to greet his brothers, and as he talked with them, he heard Goliath give his ultimatum. Goliath's conditions were clear, the stakes were high, and everyone, when they saw the man, fled from him and was afraid.

It is at this point in the narrative that some rather interesting information is made known. Apparently, King Saul offered a reward to the man who would battle Goliath and kill him. If so, Saul would give that man great riches, his own daughter as a wife, and furthermore, he would exempt the man's father from paying taxes in Israel. It was a pretty sweet deal, but alas, no takers. No one wanted to face the giant.

Whether David was interested in the reward is suspect, but David certainly disdained Goliath and repeatedly stated "What shall be done for the man who kills this Philistine and takes away the reproach from Israel? For who is this uncircumcised Philistine, that he should defy the armies of the living God" (1 Samuel 17:26, ESV). David's demeanor and statement did not sit well with Eliab, his older brother.

Perhaps feeling the sting of being rejected as king in favor of his younger brother, or reflecting his own jealous heart, Eliab angrily lashed out at David. He said, "Why have you come down? And with whom have you left those few sheep in the wilderness? I know your presumption and the evil of your heart, for you have come down to see the battle" (1 Samuel 17:28, ESV). David reacted in total surprise and stated, "What have I done now? Was it not but a word?" And he turned away from him toward another and spoke in the same way, and the people answered him again as before" (1 Samuel 17:29–30, ESV). David's mind was on the giant and the conflict at hand.

Eventually, Saul sent for David. David told the king, "Let no man's heart fail because of him. Your servant will go and fight with this Philistine" (1 Samuel 17:32, ESV). Saul was incredulous! He said, "You are not able to go against this Philistine to fight with him, for you are but a youth, and he has been a man of war from his youth" (1 Samuel 17:33, ESV). What Saul said was true, but what he did not say, and which was equally true, was that there were thousands of Jewish men, including King Saul, who were men of war but who fled from the sight of Goliath. Only a shepherd boy was willing to face the conflict facing a nation. While outwardly only a youth, inwardly David's heart was dedicated to fight for God.

When a leader faces conflict, it is of little importance what his physical stature may be, or even his level of responsibility. What matters is his desire to do what is right. His need to do the right thing supersedes the circumstances around him. It does not matter if those circumstances are found on a battlefield or in a boardroom. This was David's perspective. This must be ours.

David replied to the king that he had faced many dangers as a shepherd. He had encountered wild predators attacking the flock. He fought them, defeated them, and rescued the endangered lamb from them. Goliath would be no different.

However, David was not solely relying upon his experiences as a shepherd in facing the giant; he was relying upon God. In 1 Samuel 7.37 (ESV) he says, "The LORD who delivered me from the paw of the lion and from the paw of the bear will deliver me from the hand of this Philistine." And Saul said to David, "Go, and the LORD be with you."

David's desire to honor God, along with his dependence upon God, displayed his heart-centered leadership for God. Regardless of the challenge, David bravely faced Goliath, trusting in God to deliver him. David would not accommodate conflict whether it was a lion, a bear, or a giant. Rather, he would boldly face the conflict in full assurance that God would be honored and glorified through His servant.

When conflict occurs, people have many ideas on how to face it. Rather than depending upon God for deliverance, people often look to man-made means to accomplish what only God can do. Consequently, often man's means violate the moral standards of God's word revealing a lack of trust in God and His truth.

A couple of years after I became a senior pastor, the church began a building program. The need was great, and the time was right for such a venture. It was decided to enlist the assistance of an evangelical stewardship organization to provide direction concerning the raising of funds for the project. Many of the ideas the company representative provided were wise and insightful.

However, when it came time to challenge the congregation concerning their sacrificial giving to the project, the company's representative strongly directed me to publically reveal what my family and I were giving in order to challenge the families in the church to give proportionately more. This I would not do. Not only did I believe such counsel to be in violation of the principles outlines in 2 Corinthians 8–9 (ESV), but I also believed it smacked of pragmatism.

Upon my refusal to comply, the stewardship representative chided me for not following his counsel. He warned that were the church to not follow his advice, then the proposed project's giving would be less than what he projected.

With unwavering support from the church board and the congregation, I did not conform to the representative's counsel. I brought the proposed cost of the project to the congregation, explained the need, challenged the people to give, and led the church in prayer for God's blessing and guidance.

What happened then was pretty remarkable. The proposed financial goal was met. Pledges were collected, giving was faithful, and the structure was completed. Additionally, the church's ministry giving did not suffer. Within seven years of dedication, the church mortgage was paid off, and the church remains debt free. As was the case with us, so it was with David.

Saul sought to outfit David with all manner of armor and equipment. "Then Saul clothed David with his armor. He put a helmet of bronze on his head and clothed him with a coat of mail" (1 Samuel 17:38, ESV). However, when David fastened his sword to his armor and tried to walk, he could not. David said to Saul, "I cannot go with these, for I have not tested them." So David put them off" (1 Samuel 17:39, ESV).

David took a shepherd's tools, equipment he knew best and which God would bless. He took his staff, selected five smooth stones from the brook, and put them in his shepherd's bag. The shepherd's tools would be sufficient for God's work.

1 Samuel 17:40 (ESV) states that David "drew near to the Philistine." Facing his conflict, using the equipment God gave him, and depending upon the Lord in correctly using the tools, David was ready for battle. Any leader must meet conflict head on with the same perspective. He must never accommodate conflict, he must use the equipment God has chosen to give him, and he must depend upon the Lord by using those God given tools righteously and honorably. These tools include God's word, prayer, wise counsel, and an unflinching commitment to glorify God.

As David drew near to Goliath, the "Philistine moved forward and came near to David, with his shield-bearer in front of him" (1 Samuel 17:41, ESV). Goliath was ready to meet David on the field of battle and was utterly confident he would be victorious, indicated by his open disdain of his opponent. In 1 Samuel 17:43 (ESV) he said, "Am I a dog, that you come to me with sticks?" And the Philistine cursed David by his gods (1 Samuel 17:43, ESV). In addition, he said to David, "Come to me, and I will give your flesh to the birds of the air and to the beasts of the field" (1 Samuel 17:44, ESV).

David's response revealed his heart. Rather than being intimidated by the conflict or trusting in his equipment, he trusted in the Lord. He told the Philistine that God would deliver him into David's hand. The giant would die, and the result would not only be victory for Israel, but glory for the One, True God. David understood then what leaders need to understand today: the battle belongs to Lord.

The resources an influential leader draws power from must not be his own but rather God's. Three times David invokes God's name declaring to Goliath that by the Lord he came to him, the Lord would conquer him, and the Lord would give Goliath into Israel's hands. That is exactly what happened.

David took a smooth stone, slung it from his sling, and struck Goliath right between the eyes. The giant was killed. David was victorious. God was glorified. David defeated the giant conflict facing him. Furthermore, Israel routed the Philistine army. Israel experienced a great victory and witnessed the emergence of a great leader who would become king. David would not accommodate Goliath, as many previously had, and the result was that God delivered the giant into David's hands.

Godly leaders must never accommodate those creating conflict. Israel accommodated Goliath for more than a month, and instead of leaving, he became bolder. Today, those creating conflict must be confronted, as Goliath was, by a leader dependent upon the Lord, as David was. The result was God is glorified as He works through His chosen leader who readily takes up the battle and confronts the enemy. Nothing else is acceptable.

Sadly, 2 Samuel 11–12 (ESV) records that David's life would not stay on this righteous path but take a tragic turn when he would compromise his heart's integrity for a moment of lustful pleasure with another man's wife. David's conscious compromise did not end with one evening of adulterous passion but degenerated into deception and ultimately murder. David forfeited God's unique blessing for the rest of his life, and his family encountered multiple tragedies as a result. How could this happen to a man after God's own heart? Simple, David failed to guard his heart. He accommodated his lust and compromised.

The seeds for David's compromise occurred long before he gazed upon Bathsheba. The Scriptures record in 1 Samuel 3:2–5 (ESV) and 5:13–16 (ESV) that David was a polygamist who had multiple children by multiple wives. Wherein these marriages reflected treaties between Israel and other nations, this was in direct violation of Deuteronomy 17:17 (ESV) where God commanded Israel's future kings to refrain from having multiple wives, "lest his heart turn away, nor shall he acquire for himself excessive silver and gold" (Deuteronomy 17:17, ESV). David disobeyed God's law, resulting in disastrous consequences.

David's tragic accommodation occurred subtly. 2 Samuel 11:1 (ESV) says, "In the spring of the year, the time when kings go out to battle, David sent Joab, and his servants with him, and all Israel. And they ravaged the Ammonites and besieged Rabbah. But David remained at Jerusalem."

Notice the almost casual statement: David remained at Jerusalem. It was unusual for David to stay home from battle. He should have been with his army but chose instead to relax at home. This was his first mistake.

So it goes with leaders today. A seemingly insignificant choice can produce devastating consequences. Often these consequences are neither anticipated nor considered. However, they are real. A casual glance, an ignored discipline, or a neglected decision can bring incalculable misery. This is where the damage begins but not where it ends.

"It happened, late one afternoon, when David arose from his couch and was walking on the roof of the king's house, that he saw from the roof a woman bathing; and the woman was very beautiful" (2 Samuel 11:2, ESV). David saw a woman bathing. Within the context, the word "saw" means "to gaze." David did not take a casual glance but rather gazed for some time. Lust was rising up within his heart. Numbers 15:39 (ESV) states "remember all the commandments of the LORD, to do them, not to follow after your own heart and your own eyes, which you are inclined to whore after" (Numbers 15:39, ESV).

The text said the woman was very beautiful to behold. Notice the adjective "very." This woman was extraordinarily beautiful. Additionally, she was bathing. She was without clothing. She was naked. There was not much left to David's imagination. He was aroused. He wanted her. David did not guard his eyes.

This is one of the most important lessons a leader can learn when working or serving with the opposite sex. Guard your eyes! Always be consciously aware of any instance when your eyes begin to wander. It takes determination to be this disciplined. However, the rewards are huge if you do. Likewise, the consequences are just as huge if you do not.

What followed was a disintegration of righteousness, which happened with such abandon that David's brazenness is shocking. He sent for the woman (2 Samuel 11:3, ESV) and found out she was married (11:3b ESV). He had sex with her (11:4 ESV), and she became pregnant (11:5 ESV). Along with not guarding his eyes, David did not guard his steps.

A roving eye can lead to roaming feet. What is initially considered can lead to consummation. What David did not consider, and what leaders must always recognize, is that what we think is what we are or what we will become.

David's character became irrevocably shattered. The tragedy was that he was the one responsible for shattering it. He ceased being a man of integrity. He ceased being a man after God's own heart.

Unfortunately, this was not the end of David's downward slide into accommodation. David perpetuated his sin by seeking to cover it up. He called for Bathsheba's husband, Uriah the Hittite, to come home from the battlefield. Feigning interest in the military conflict, David was only concerned in manipulating Uriah into spending the evening with Bathsheba. Therefore, the pregnancy would naturally be attributed to him.

However, Uriah did not comply. When David asked why, Uriah replied, "The ark and Israel and Judah dwell in booths, and my lord Joab and the servants of my lord are camping in the open field. Shall I then go to my house, to eat and to drink and to lie with my wife? As you live, and as your soul lives, I will not do this thing" (2 Samuel 11:11, ESV). David did not guard his mouth from deceit or his lips from perversity.

The leader's failure to guard his eyes leads to failure to guard his steps. This can lead to him failing to guard his mouth. He attempts to dismiss what happened. He may deny anything happened. He may lie about what happened.

Uriah's integrity is outstanding while David's pales in comparison. Rather than follow Uriah's example, David continued to manipulate by getting Uriah drunk in the hopes that the honorable soldier would cast off restraint and be passionate with his wife. Again, this Uriah would not do.

Therefore, David continued his downward slide by hitting rock bottom. He arranged for Uriah to be killed in battle. David would now be able to marry Bathsheba, and no one would be the wiser. David failed to remove his foot from evil.

When the leader does not confess his sin, it leads to more sin. When he chooses to not see his sin as God sees it, then the leader will continue his downward spiral until he crashes. For David, lust led to lewd behavior. This led to lying. It culminated in premeditated murder.

It is ironic that the young shepherd boy who would not accommodate a giant Philistine warrior representing unrighteousness lost his own personal integrity as king by accommodating unrighteousness within his own life. David's experience shows leaders that while conflict often occurs from outside sources, the man of God must always be aware of the ever present conflict within his own soul.

The incident concludes with this statement: "And when the mourning was over, David sent and brought her to his house, and she became his wife and bore him a son. But the thing that David had done displeased the Lord" (2 Samuel 11:27, ESV). David may have thought he had gotten away with murder, but God was watching. He was watching David. He is watching us.

God's name had not occurred throughout David's sordid affair. It does in 2 Samuel 12:1 when God confronts David with his sin. "And the Lord sent Nathan to David" (2 Samuel 12:1, ESV).

Nathan was a prophet of God during David's and Solomon's reign. 1 Kings 4:5 (ESV) records that two of Nathan sons served in King Solomon's court. 2 Chronicles 29 (ESV) states that Nathan developed temple music and wrote an account of David's and Solomon's respective rule.

In 2 Samuel 7:1–17 (ESV), God told Nathan that Solomon would build the temple and not David. In 1 Kings 1:5–48 (ESV), God used Nathan to ensure Solomon's succession to the throne upon David's death. David forfeited his integrity, but God had Nathan.

In 2 Samuel 12:2–4 (ESV), Nathan came to David and told a simple story about two men. One was wealthy, the other poor. Wealth was often determined by how much livestock an individual owned. The wealthy man had many flocks and herds. The poor had but one, little ewe lamb. The lamb was more a pet than a possession. It was like a member of the man's family.

One day, a visitor arrived at the rich man's home. It was an appropriate custom to provide the rich man's visitor a feast as a display of hospitality. However, rather than kill one of his own animals for dinner, the rich man took the poor man's one ewe lamb and slew it instead.

Upon hearing the story, "David's anger was greatly kindled against the man, and he said to Nathan, 'As the LORD lives, the man who has done this deserves to die, and he shall restore the lamb fourfold, because he did this thing, and because he had no pity'" (2 Samuel 12:5–6, ESV).

David's righteous anger is striking. He had no idea that Nathan meant him. Nathan's response to David was calculatedly cold: "You are the man" (2 Samuel 12:7, ESV).

The Scriptures do not tell us what David's initial reaction was, but we know that Nathan did not stop with this single pronouncement. He unloaded both barrels expressing God's anger. He spoke to David about all the privileges God had given him: the wealth and the wives. If that had not been enough, God would have given him more. Yet David spurned God's generosity and plunged himself into immorality, deception, and murder.

Nathan was not finished. After expressing God's displeasure, he then announced God's judgment. Violence would never leave David's family. In fact, David would face insurrection and revolt emanating from his own children. Additionally, what David did in secret would happen to him publically. He would be shamed, humiliated, and hunted. Finally, the four-fold judgment David pronounced would fall upon his children. Four of his offspring would die.

The word "adversity" is from the Hebrew הָעַר (*ra'*) meaning "evil, affliction, calamity, displeasure, and misery." God would bring judgmental adversity and conflict into David's life, for the rest of his life, as a consequence of David ignoring the conflict of sin within his soul.

David acknowledged his sin in response to Nathan's confrontation. David said, "I have sinned against the LORD" (2 Samuel 12:13, ESV). However, the adversity Nathan spoke of would soon come when Nathan said, "The LORD also has put away your sin; you shall not die. Nevertheless, because by this deed you have utterly scorned the LORD, the child who is born to you shall die." Then Nathan went to his house. And the LORD afflicted the child that Uriah's wife bore to David, and he became sick" (2 Samuel 12:13–15, ESV). What a heavy price to pay by failing to confront conflict within one's own life.

The irony here is that the shepherd boy who would not allow a pagan giant to blaspheme the name of the Lord became a king who would perpetrate such sin as to cause God's enemies to blaspheme His holy name. Oh, how great was David's fall!

Why did God not prevent David from his consummate slide into accommodation and sin? Why did God permit David to sin resulting in judgment, not only upon himself, but also his family? Why did God not intervene sooner?

Perhaps the answer lies in God showing not only David, but future leaders, the devastating consequences when a leader accommodates conflict, especially his soul's battle with temptation and sin. Perhaps the answer is that God will always raise another leader to confront the sin of His anointed, be it a king, priest, or pastor. Nathan the priest was just such a man.

David's victory over Goliath, and his crushing defeat with himself, offer valuable lessons yet today on a leader's development, lessons which must not be ignored. These are lessons that remain timeless truths regarding what it takes to have the heart of a great leader.

- Watch out for the small, seemingly insignificant accommodations to temptation.
- One compromise with temptation and sin can lead to further compromises with temptation and sin. The cycle will continue.
- The leader must always be prepared and never let his guard down. To do so cannot only be dangerous but deadly.
- Once character has been compromised, even a little, it is hard to retrieve. The fallen leader lives with his shame for the rest of his life. There is no escaping it.

CHAPTER EIGHT

Theoretical Foundations and Theological Conclusions Concerning Conflict

Trials! All humans have them. All sinners experience them, whether through the consequences of their own decisions or someone else's. The book of Job reminds believers that trials, especially conflicts, are inevitable: "For affliction does not come from the dust, nor does trouble sprout from the ground, but man is born to trouble as the sparks fly upward" (Job 5:6–7, ESV).

In examining the theme of the indispensability of conflict in the development of godly, leadership, the crucible of conflict has also affected historical characters who became leaders indispensable for their time. What can be learned from their encounters with conflict while leading a church, an army, or a nation? How did their respective experiences of rejection, hardship, and war shape and mold them into becoming leaders who are now admired, respected, and emulated? I submit three individuals for consideration: Jonathan Edwards, George Washington, and Sir Winston Churchill. While not all professed a trust in Jesus Christ, the leadership qualities they exemplified due to conflict should encourage the godly leader in the ongoing development to lead.

Jonathan Edwards (1703–1758) was an American theologian and congregational clergyman whom God used to stir the religious revival called the Great Awakening in America during the early eighteenth century. Edwards was born October 5, 1703, in the colony of East Windsor, Connecticut. His parents were Timothy and Esther (Stoddard) Edwards. Timothy Edwards served as a pastor in East Windsor.

Jonathan Edwards was a brilliant man and one God used immediately. He entered Yale University at thirteen and graduated as class valedictorian. He would eventually earn his master's degree from the same institution. It was also during this time that he preached at a church and tutored other students. He was ordained in 1727 and became an assistant to his grandfather, Samuel Stoddard, who pastured a church at Northampton, Massachusetts Bay Colony.

After his grandfather died, Edwards became pastor at Northampton at age twenty-six. In spite of the growing trend toward Arminian theology in the New England colonies, Edwards remained a firm Calvinist and an ardent believer in the doctrine of election. His first public refutation of Arminianism was in 1731 in a sermon entitled *God Glorified in Man's Dependence.*

God sovereignly used Jonathan Edwards through his preaching. In 1734–1735, a revival occurred in Northampton resulting in a significant number of conversions. Three hundred new members joined Edwards's church. Together with Evangelist George Whitefield, Edwards became a significant tool for God in the New England revival known as The Great Awakening. It was during this period that Edwards preached his most famous sermon *Sinners in the Hands of an Angry God.*

The Great Awakening made a significant impact in Edwards's church and upon Edwards. He continually stressed a strong commitment to Christ in living and glorifying Him. However, there were those who objected not only to The Great Awakening in general, but also to Edwards's fervency for congregational holiness in particular.

Edwards strongly objected to the Halfway Covenant, which was a "New England church custom that permitted a baptized person to have all the privileges of church membership although they had not openly professed conversion" (Edwards, par. 5). Edwards passionately believed that not only was a public profession of Christianity necessary for church membership but also that a public profession of faith in Christ should impact one's behavior in striving to live a holy life. "His whole case is that the church must not allow a separation between a profession of Christ and conduct which supports that profession, because a profession of the essence of Christianity which should be required of candidates includes such truths as repentance and gospel holiness" (Murray, 336).

The resulting conflict between Edwards and those who embraced the Halfway Covenant resulted in Edwards's dismissal as pastor of Northampton in 1750. As Iain Murray explains, "Even though he saw it coming, and could speak so calmly in his *Farewell Sermon*, Edwards was undoubtedly shocked by the strangeness and the finality of his dismissal" (Murray, 333).

In writing to a colleague in Scotland regarding his dismissal, Edwards stated, "I am now separated from the people between whom and me there was once the greatest union. Remarkable is the providence of God in the matter. In this event we have the striking instance of the instability and uncertainty of all things here below" (Murray, 333). Edwards displayed a trust in a holy

God that His sovereign plan was perfect, even though sinful, imperfect men carried it to completion.

As Murray explains, "There is little doubt that the existing prejudices of tradition, backed by the misrepresentations stirred up by leaders in the church and some who Edwards calls "crafty designing men" account for the sad way in which many Christians acted" (Murray, 340). Edwards wrote, "The great power of prejudices from education, established custom, and the traditions of ancestors and certain admired teachers, and the exceeding unhappy influence of bigotry, has remarkably appeared in the management of this affair" (Murray, 340).

Edwards believed that the underlying sin concerning his dismissal was the Northampton church's pride and his "fundamental explanation of what had happened was that God permitted such weaknesses in order to expose the evil of spiritual pride" (Murray, 341). Edwards was convinced that the congregation's increasing wealth and reputation, along with its tutelage under Edwards, fueled its arrogance against its own shepherd. Edwards further stated that:

> Spiritual pride is a most monstrous thing. If it be not discerned and vigorously opposed, in the beginning, it very often soon raises persons above their teachers, and supposed spiritual fathers, and sets them out of the reach of all rule and instruction, as I have seen in innumerable instances. (Murray, 341)

However, Edwards learned much through this ordeal. He admitted his failures as a pastor, which he believed contributed to his eventual dismissal. These failures included:

- Not visiting the sick unless called upon to do so. Edwards was not prone to call upon church members unless called upon. Unfortunately, this fostered an impression that he was aloof and more concerned with his studies than God's people
- His failure as a teacher. Edwards failed to understand the congregation's tendency to accept a person's profession of conversion rather than the evidences of conversion.
- His immaturity during the critical, early years of his ministry. As with any leader, Edwards grew by the experiences of life and leadership. He acknowledged his lack of judgment and discernment undermined the people's confidence in him.

While Edwards candidly admitted his failures, he also held two strong convictions of which he would not compromise. First, he recognized the serious nature of the issue regarding a communicant's sincere profession of biblical, saving faith in Jesus Christ. "There was never any hesitation in Edwards' mind over the serious nature of the truth involved. He came to the firm conviction that a wrong principle of admission to the Lord's Table imperils the whole nature of the church, for then the world and the church cease to be distinguished" (Murray, 347).

Second, when Edwards's chief opponent in the controversy at Northampton, Joseph Hawley, wrote Edwards years later and expressed his repentance and grief over his role in Edwards's dismissal, Edwards responded with graciousness to his cousin and "with true candor and Christian charity" (Murray, 348). Edwards wrote:

> I have had enough of this controversy and desire to have done with it. I have spent enough of the precious time of

> my life in it heretofore. I desire and pray that God may enable you to view things truly, and as He views them, and so to act in the affair as shall be best for you, and most for your peace living and dying. (Murray, 348)

Following his dismissal, Edwards pastored a village church in Stockbridge, Massachusetts. While serving on the frontier, he also ministered to the Housatonic Indians. While he ministered, he wrote some of the most famous theological works ever written in America. "Among them was *A Careful and Strict Inquiry into the Notions of the Freedom of the Will (1754)*, in which he denied that human beings have self-determined will that can initiate acts not known or decreed beforehand by God" (Edwards, par. 5).

In 1757, Edwards accepted the presidency of the College of New Jersey, which would become Princeton University. However, five weeks after his installation he died as a result of an inoculation against smallpox, which was then epidemic in the American colonies.

Edwards's experience in Northampton teaches leaders today that conflict can arise even after decades of effective leadership and service. It does not matter who you are, even an individual as respected as Jonathan Edwards. When a leader stands for principle, he may find himself standing alone with only the Lord at his side. However, that is sufficient.

Edward's also illustrated that a leader must be willing to admit his mistakes, learn from his mistakes, and not harbor bitterness because of the consequences indirectly caused by his mistakes. Leaders must be willing to humble themselves in order to eventually overcome their errors.

Edwards exemplified the fact that even after great difficulties and disappointment, a leader can serve and minister again in new and different ways. Leaders may not always have the same responsibilities, but they can continue to become better leaders with their new responsibilities.

Finally, Edwards acknowledged the truth that God is always in control.

The conflicts involving American colonial churches would eventually give way to an even greater series of widespread political difficulties and trials, resulting in the colonies declaring independence from Great Britain in 1776. Many colonists rose to prominent positions of colonial leadership during this period, but none greater than Virginia planter George Washington.

George Washington (1732–1799) remains to this day a leader who transcends his time. His ability to lead an army under the most difficult of circumstances, while fighting a superior military force, cannot be overemphasized or ignored. During the Revolutionary War, the Colonial Army's wintering at Valley Forge, Pennsylvania, in 1777–1778 remains a true example of how conflict develops leadership and how an assorted assembly of revolutionaries became an army.

Washington's leadership during this period was incredible and not to be minimized. Encountering great hardships, many problems, and overwhelming odds, he founded and fostered a group of unorganized farmers, craftsman, and laborers into an army that defeated the British. Following an eight-year conflict (1775–1783), the Continental Army achieved final victory at Yorktown, Virginia. The colonies had won its independence.

George Washington was born in Westmoreland County, Virginia, on February 22, 1732. He was the eldest son of a well-to-do Virginia farmer, Augustine Washington, by his second wife, Mary Ball. The Washington family rose to wealth and prosperity as the result of steady application to farming, land buying, and development of local industries.

Young George grew rapidly in physical stature and maturity. His emotional maturity was probably due to his father's death when George was eleven, his elder brother Lawrence's death when George was eighteen, and his numerous experiences in the American wilderness.

The conflicts a leader encounters may toughen him or break him. If it breaks him, the possibility for future leadership opportunities will be few. However, if the leader emerges stronger, more resilient, and mentally sharper for having encountered conflict, there will be little he will not be able to accomplish.

Washington's trials as a young man tested him severely, but he became a man who possessed tremendous physical and mental strength. His personal integrity became unquestionable. He was not bothered by criticism, lack of supplies, or failure. His early years of maturing would prepare him for the greater challenges ahead. So do ours!

Washington served as an officer in the British army during England's conflict with France known as the French and Indian War (1754–1763). He encountered several massacres, an embarrassing defeat, and a hollow victory. Historian Joseph Ellis, in describing Washington's character, states:

> Whether it was a miracle, destiny, or sheer luck, he had emerged from these traumatic experiences unscathed and with his reputation, each time, higher than before.
>
> His courage, his composure, and his self-control were all of a piece, having developed within that highly lethal environment that was the Ohio Country, where internal shields provided the only defense against dangers that came at you from multiple angles. What will in later years be regarded as an arrogant aloofness began in his young

> manhood as a wholly protective urge to establish space around himself that bullets, insults, and criticism could never penetrate. Because he lacked both the presumptive superiority of a British aristocrat and the economic resources of a Tidewater grandee, Washington could only rely on the hard core of his own merit. (Ellis, 38)

The conflicts Washington encountered in his young adulthood would serve him in good stead when upon reaching his later years, he would face the daunting task of the imposing British army while serving as the commander in chief of the Continental Army of America in the War for Independence. Washington did not lead a standing army. His troops consisted of volunteers who served for a period of time from various colonies. While Washington was busily leading one army, he was at the same time, of necessity, recruiting another one to take its place.

Numerous battles ensued between the makeshift colonial army and the more disciplined and experienced British regulars. Stunning victories by the Americans were immediately followed by equally stunning defeats. However, America's fight for independence chronicled not only the character of a nation but also its leadership.

> The American Revolution was the central event in Washington's life, the crucible for his development as a mature man, a prominent statesman, and a national hero. In effect, the character of the man and the character of the nation congealed and grew together during the extended moment of eight years. (Ellis, 73)

The indispensability of God-ordained conflict in developing leadership especially expressed itself in the horrific winter of

1777–1778 where Washington and his troops, at Valley Forge, Pennsylvania, endured great hardships and emerged with great fortitude and strength of purpose the following spring. During colonial times, armies in conflict would cease combat during the winter months. What is inconceivable today was a common tactic of warfare two hundred and fifty years ago. British General William Howe's army passed the winter in fairly comfortable quarters in Philadelphia. Washington's army wintered under conditions of extreme privation at Valley Forge, where they could observe any move Howe madc. Historians conclude that the Continental Army's wintering of 1777–1778 at Valley Forge forged in them a perseverance resulting from the trials and conflict they experienced. As one historian writes:

> The Continental Army's encampment at Valley Forge in Pennsylvania during the winter of 1777-1778 was the bleakest time of the American struggle for independence. Hunger and disease compounded the problems of inadequate shelter and lack of adequate winter clothing. More than 2500 men died of typhus, dysentery, and pneumonia. Washington made repeated appeals for aid and supplies, but the Congress was unable to move the states to provide them. (Washington, par. 51)

Jeff Shaara, in his book *The Glorious Cause*, ponders what Washington must have thought as the bleakness of that winter eventually gave way to the warmth of spring. He explains:

> What army in Europe would endure what these men have suffered? In Europe, this army would have simply dissolved into great bloody riots. They would come here as a mob, would have destroyed this place, taken every

> scrap of clothing and food, stolen every boot, and if the officers could not escape, they would be hanged. But the Americans…simply endure. If this army prevails in this war, it may be by the very suffering they have endured here, by their very survival. It is as if they understand that their cause is more important than their suffering. The British will never understand that. (Shaara, 363)

As Joseph Ellis contemplates:

> It is not clear how many men died of disease and exposure at Valley Forge, but new recruits and, even more important, reenlistments "for the duration," bolstered the size of the army to twelve thousand in March 1778, with a core of about five thousand battle-tested veterans. And more were on the way. One of the dominant themes in Washington's early life had been the elemental fact that success followed survival. His military reputation following the Braddock debacle, his inheritance of Mount Vernon, his marriage to Martha Custis, all had occurred when others fell by the wayside and he was left standing. If Washington regarded the Continental army as the institutional projection of his own personality, then the troops marching out of winter quarters at Valley Forge in May 1778 represented a new chapter in that same elemental story. (Ellis, 118)

Survival! Endurance! Self-Control! These qualities embedded themselves into Washington's character throughout his life but especially as a result of his experiences at Valley Forge. He emerged from that trial and conflict to lead the colonies to independence and eventually to become the new-nation's first president. However, it was his sheer determination in leading the

Continental army to victory which remains one of Washington's greatest legacies of leadership.

What experiences have you encountered that have resulted in a greater endurance and self-control in your character? While they were not easy to survive, survive you have and survive you will in order to emerge a seasoned and toughened veteran of leadership. The more conflicts a leader faces the more resilient he becomes. Such a resilient leader was Sir Winston Churchill.

Keeping a lone nation in existence from the military threat of Nazi Germany, 160 years after the American Revolution, would become Winston Churchill's greatest legacy of leadership for the cause of freedom. No other leader did as much during the Second World War to ensure the defeat of tyranny, and no other twentieth-century leader experienced as much disappointment and conflict in his life as Churchill. However, it was through the conflicts he encountered as a youth and young adult that he was prepared to lead England during the turbulent 1940s.

Sir Winston Leonard Spencer Churchill (1874–1965) was a man of two centuries. He was born in the nineteenth-century splendor of Queen Victoria's unprecedented sixty-three-year reign (1837–1901) of the United Kingdom. This was when Great Britain, which included Canada, Australia, India, New Zealand, and large parts of Africa, was the most powerful nation on earth. Churchill lived well into the twentieth century and witnessed the advent of two world wars, a world-wide economic depression, mass mechanization, fascism, growing telecommunications, the development and use of nuclear energy, the rise and spread of Communism, and the Phoenix-like rebirth, following Japan's surprise attack at Pearl Harbor, of the inarguable military and economic might of the United States, which far eclipsed his own beloved England.

He was a renaissance man—author, speaker, journalist, politician, painter, and warrior. Churchill held every important cabinet office in the British government, except foreign minister. He was known "for the many books on British history and politics he wrote throughout his lifetime and his command of the English language not only made him a great orator but earned him the Nobel Prize for literature in 1953" (Churchill, par. 2). However, World War II, and especially its early days, afforded Churchill his "finest hour" of leadership. This greatest of conflicts the modern world has ever witnessed, saw in Churchill one of the greatest leaders history has ever recorded.

Churchill seemed destined to be a man who did not flee from conflict. Whether as a war correspondent, a soldier, a member of Parliament, or even as Prime Minister of England, he savored battle. Some historians question whether he enjoyed war too much. William Manchester explains that Churchill denied this charge and called war a "dirty, shoddy businesses…disguise it as you may" (Manchester, 10). However, when war was necessary, and against Nazi Germany it was, Churchill was ready and willing to do battle to the death, if necessary. This was certainly the case at the time of the English evacuation of Dunkirk. Manchester states:

> The French had collapsed, The Dutch had been overwhelmed. The Belgians had surrendered. The British army, trapped, fought free and fell back toward the Channel ports, converging on a fishing town whose name was then spelled Dunkerque. Behind them lay the sea. It was England's greatest crisis since the Norman Conquest, vaster than those precipitated by Phillip II's Spanish Armada, Louis XIV's triumphant armies, or Napoleon's invasion barges massed at Boulogne. This time Britain

> stood alone. If the Germans crossed the Channel and established uncontested beachheads, all would be lost. (Manchester, 3)

Following the miraculous and successful evacuation of 338,682 British and French troops from Dunkirk by trawlers, tugs, scows, fishing sloops, lifeboats, and pleasure crafts, England needed a new leader who would face the slaughtering blitzkrieg of Adolf Hitler's crushing forces and lead a free people to victory. The accommodation with Germany by England's former Prime Minister Neville Chamberlain had failed. "England's new leader, were he to prevail, would have to stand for everything England's decent, civilized establishment had rejected" (Manchester, 4). Winston Churchill was just such a man.

Churchill was despised by many within Parliament, especially after becoming prime minister. His predecessor detested him and everything he stood for. Even Hitler thought that he would be able to reason with him. Many leaders in England thought that one last appeasement with Germany was the only way England would survive and achieve peace. It was the only course of action a reasonable man could conclude.

However, Churchill was not a reasonable man. To his war cabinet, Churchill said:

> I have thought carefully in these last days whether it was part of my duty to consider entering into negotiations with that man and concluded that if this long island story of ours is to end at last, let it end only when each one of us lies choking in his own blood upon the ground. I have nothing to offer but blood, toil, tears, and sweat.

Churchill continued:

> Even though large tracts of Europe and many old and famous states have fallen or may fall into the grip of the Gestapo and all the odious apparatus of Nazi rule, we shall not flag nor fail. We shall go on to the end. We shall fight in France, we shall fight on the seas and oceans, we shall fight with growing confidence and growing strength in the air, we shall defend our island, whatever the cost may be, we shall fight on the beaches, we shall fight on the landing grounds, we shall fight in the fields and in the streets, we shall fight in the hills; we shall never surrender.

Churchill's indomitable will, his refusal to compromise with evil, and his ability to inspire the people he led conjoined during those dark and conflict filled days of 1940. He was the leader England needed at that time of conflict and because it would be another eighteen months before America officially entered the war, he was the leader the free world needed.

Manchester called Churchill the Last Lion because of his extraordinary courage. On his eightieth birthday, Churchill stated, "It was the nation and the race dwelling all round the globe that had the lion's heart; I had the luck to be called upon to give the roar" (Manchester, 7).

Do you have the courage to be like a lion? Are you willing to stand alone when it is necessary knowing that to do otherwise would compromise your character, impugn your integrity, and cause all you have stood for to be called into question? Extraordinary situations call for extraordinary leaders to display extraordinary courage. While your circumstances may not necessarily equal those Churchill encountered, are you equal to the challenges you will face? This is the question facing all leaders and it can only be answered when the leader stares into the blackness of the abyss and emerges victorious.

Trials and conflicts occur in the lives of leaders. However, believers in Jesus Christ are to rejoice in the midst of trials and to face them with joy. Joy in a trial! How is this for a contradiction of terms? How is this possible? Joy is "extreme gladness and a vivid emotion of pleasure" (Oxford, 438). A trial is "a judicial examination; a process of testing qualities; a test; a hardship or trouble" (Oxford, 886). How can there be pleasure in trouble? How can there be gladness in hardship? In what way can these two concepts possibly agree? What is their purpose if they are in agreement? On the surface, nothing would seem to be farther from the truth than these two polar opposite terms coinciding.

What is the worst trial or conflict you could ever encounter? It might be losing your job. It could be failing to find a new job. What about the death of a child or a parent? It might be the sudden destruction of your home to a hurricane or a tornado. Regardless of what it could be, or has been, God permits these incidents: not to necessarily punish us but rather to refine us to become more like Him. Therein is the joy in the midst of conflict. Through it all, leaders become more like Jesus.

An individual with an unbiblical worldview would perhaps laugh and scorn at such a proposition of facing trials with joy. However, God is not silent regarding the subject. In fact, He explicitly addresses the issue in the New Testament book of James.

James wrote the following paradoxical statement in chapter 1:2–4 (ESV): "Count it all joy, my brothers, when you meet trials of various kinds, for you know that the testing of your faith produces steadfastness. And let steadfastness have its full effect, that you may be perfect and complete, lacking in nothing." Examining this text in detail will yield rich doctrinal truth regarding the thesis of God using conflict to develop godly leaders.

James identified himself as "a servant of God and of the Lord Jesus Christ" (James 1:1, ESV). His letter was directed "To the twelve tribes in the Dispersion: Greetings" (James 1:1, ESV).

"My brothers!" (James 1:2, ESV). To whom was James writing? The consensus is that James wrote to believers because "the nature of the imperatives could only be directed at believers" (Gromacki, 338). He probably addressed first-century Jewish Christians scattered from their homes due to the persecution for their faith by unbelieving Jews and Romans. This persecution may have occurred immediately following Stephen's martyrdom (Acts 8:1–4; 11:19, ESV) and been accentuated by Herod Agrippa I (Acts 12, ESV). However, the title "brothers" also applies to all believers in Christ, then and now. Therefore, the promises and premises contained in the epistle are pertinent and applicable to all believers in Christ.

James continued by writing, "Count it all joy" (James 1:2, ESV). Christians are commanded to continually count, "to lead, to think, to believe, or to regard" (Kittel, 303) it all joy. What is joy? Joy means to be "rejoicing" and to have "merriness" (Kittel, 1299). It is from the Greek word "χαρά" (*chara*), a derivative for the word "grace."

James then stated, "Count it all joy, my brothers, when you meet trials of various kinds" (James 1:2, ESV). Notice the word "when." It is not a question of "if" a believer will encounter trials but rather a question of "when." The text is saying that trials will come. They are inevitable. The personal pronoun "you" indicates a personal truth that each Christian will fall into or experience trials. Believers may face trials through no fault of their own. This concept is conveyed in the "Parable of the Good Samaritan" when a certain man fell among thieves (Luke 10:30, ESV).

"The word trial, πειρασμός (*periosmos*), describes things that put a person to the test. They may be difficulties that come from without, such as persecution, or they may be inner moral tests, such as temptations to sin. James uses the word in the former sense in verses 2–4" (Burdick, 168).

What kind of trials will Christians experience? Various trials! The word various means "mutli-colored or manifold" (Kittel, 901). It won't be one trial, but a kaleidoscope of conflict. "Various" is from the Greek word "ποικίλος" (*poiklios*). "In the Greek of this verse the picturesque adjective *various,* or "varied" is in an emphatic position, and it would not have been wasted here by a master of the language" (Adamson, 53). Trials may be numerous and multifaceted in character. They may occur in various forms: financial, emotional, educational, physical, relational, psychological, and/or spiritual. They may appear as disappointments, frustrations, misunderstandings, unfulfilled dreams, unmet expectations, loss, loneliness, fear, criticism, and persecution. However, trials do have a positive purpose.

What positive purposes do trials present? James wrote, "For you know that the testing of your faith produces steadfastness. And let steadfastness have its full effect, that you may be perfect and complete, lacking in nothing" (James 1:3–4, ESV). Knowing means to have "intelligent comprehension" (Kittel, 119). The text teaches that believers can know presently and actively that God seeks to prove or approve the genuineness of their faith through testing.

"Tested" was often written on the underside of pottery signifying the pottery had gone through the furnace, or kiln, and had come out without cracks. "As a goldsmith, who allows the silver in the fire and the gold in the crucible to be purified no longer than necessary, so God purifies the righteous: each one according to his rank and deeds" (Adamson, 54). God's desire is for His children to come through the furnace of trials He brings with a stronger spiritual commitment, trust, dependence, and reverential fear of Him.

What do trials produce? It "produces steadfastness" (James 1:3, ESV). Steadfastness or patience is defined as "patient endurance, to stand firm, to endure, to bear" (Kittel, 582). Patience, "ὑπομονή" (*hypomonē*), "becomes a prominent virtue in the sense of courageous endurance" (Kittel, 582). The Bible speaks often concerning this endurance that God produces within His children as they abide under His sovereign care. In Psalm 40:1–3 (ESV), David writes:

> I waited patiently for the LORD; he inclined to me and heard my cry. He drew me up from the pit of destruction, out of the miry bog, and set my feet upon a rock, making my steps secure. He put a new song in my mouth, a song of praise to our God. Many will see and fear, and put their trust in the LORD.

The Apostle Paul writes in 1 Corinthians 10:13 (ESV) that:

> No temptation has overtaken you that is not common to man. God is faithful, and he will not let you be tempted beyond your ability, but with the temptation he will also provide the way of escape, that you may be able to endure it.

In 2 Thessalonians 1:2–4 (ESV), Paul writes:

> Grace to you and peace from God our Father and the Lord Jesus Christ. We ought always to give thanks to God for you, brothers, as is right, because your faith is growing abundantly, and the love of every one of you for one another is increasing. Therefore we ourselves boast about you in the churches of God for your steadfastness

> and faith in all your persecutions and in the afflictions that you are enduring.

Finally, in I Peter 1:6–9 (ESV), the apostle states:

> In this you rejoice, though now for a little while, if necessary, you have been grieved by various trials, so that the tested genuineness of your faith—more precious than gold that perishes though it is tested by fire—may be found to result in praise and glory and honor at the revelation of Jesus Christ. Though you have not seen him, you love him. Though you do not now see him, you believe in him and rejoice with joy that is inexpressible and filled with glory, obtaining the outcome of your faith, the salvation of your souls.

Through trials, God produces endurance in the Christian. Through this endurance, the Christian praises God. "And let steadfastness have its full effect, that you may be perfect and complete, lacking in nothing" (James 1:4, ESV). God gives Christians a command to make sure endurance reaches its mature, spiritual goal, or outcome. James is not referring to sinless perfection in describing this as a "perfect work" but rather the believer's spiritual progress and development. The believer is to embrace the testing from God and not shake his fist and angrily chastise the Lord for what He has permitted. Rather, the believer is to recognize God's testing results in a deeper communion, a greater trust, a well-rounded spiritual life and completeness. "Time teaches patience. So here it is not a question of more of our fruits which will give completeness of Christian character but of continued striving by God's grace to see that our endurance be unremittingly carried on to our death" (Adamson, 55).

Such trials not only produce patient endurance and maturity, but also "wisdom [James 1:5, ESV], stability [James 1:6–8, ESV], humility [James 1:10, ESV], blessing [James 1:12, ESV] and love [James 1:12, ESV] in the believer's life. Wisdom to understand the purpose of the test can be secured through believing prayer. God designs such tests for certain duration and the believer must endure it completely" (Gromacki, 341).

CHAPTER NINE

The Storm Clouds Gather

Trials not only produce patient endurance and maturity but also wisdom, stability, humility, blessing, and love in the believer's life. Commitment to this truth is indispensible amidst those gathering storm clouds of conflict. This is the biblical basis concerning John's (not his real name) own personal journey of counting it all joy in the midst of trials as God used conflict in the church to further develop him into a godly, pastoral leader. John and Jennifer are a young couple in full time ministry. John pastors a small church in the Midwest. They have three children, a mortgage, and a love for the Lord and a desire to serve Him. They are leaders who faced conflict and emerged stronger because of God's refining work.

Their story is a brief account of the firestorm John, his family, and his church encountered. We will witness the sparks of the conflict, its growth, its maturity, and the subsequent events leading to John's temporary removal from the pastorate. We will learn lessons God taught the church and John through the trial. We will see how God strengthened John and his family. We will see what smoldering, dying embers of conflict still glow. Finally, we will learn what godly leadership qualities John possesses to a greater degree.

Returning to the ministry, while signaling an immediate conclusion to the conflict, was not the culmination of the restoration process. God continues to heal John and his family even though John often feels like he is walking on eggshells. God continues to heal John's wife, Jennifer, from the hurts inflicted upon her while simultaneously developing her into an ever stronger godly leader. It is with this in mind that we now focus our attention on the conflict that occurred at their church.

The circumstances arising in the church John pastors exploded into a full-fledged conflict resulting in the church elders giving him a mandated sabbatical. Rather than just a theoretical issue, encountering and managing church conflict, having joy in trials, and growing as a godly leader became a practical reality for John.

What started the conflict? It began with a building program. Actually, that is not entirely true. The events leading to the conflict were preceded by numerous, seemingly insignificant encounters with a few, specific people of the church since John had become pastor. However, when the church began a building program, the sparks of discontent loomed ever larger and began to burn brightly.

What were those sparks? To begin with, there was what we'll call ministerial territoriality. This is the perspective that a particular area of the church building, or ministry, is the exclusive property of those using that particular area of the church building. Anyone seeking to use such facilities may do so at their so-called peril. A focal point of this attitude became the church nursery.

An individual directing the nursery ministry demonstrated the perspective that nothing regarding the nursery could occur without her approval. When the building committee made independent decisions without consulting her, which were seemingly insignificant (the transfer of baby cribs from the old building to the new, for example), she became upset. Obviously, the issue was not insignificant to her, and her anger grew and did not dissipate. In fact, it spilled over into accusations against Jennifer, who was also involved in the nursery ministry at the time. Numerous attempts were made to reconcile with the individual but to no avail.

A second spark was an accusatory spirit, which developed in the church, also against Jennifer. People found fault where she sat in church, accused her of being uncompromising and called her a liar. There were unspoken expectations of Jennifer by people within the church, which she unknowingly and obviously failed to fulfill.

A third spark was the development and establishment of the church's elementary level Christian school. The school began shortly after the congregation had moved into the new church facility. There were those, including several church leaders, who believed the school should not have started so soon after the completion of the building's construction phase. However, God clearly showed the church it was His will to proceed. Providential circumstances, answered prayer, and numerous other so-called miracles indicated to the overall church leadership that it was God's will to begin the school at that time.

Almost immediately, conflict arose between laypeople involved in the established ministries of the church and those serving in the new school. People expressed resentment in Sunday school rooms becoming school classrooms. Differences arose. A ministry territorial attitude developed regarding what church-owned equipment could and could not be used by the school. The church trustees became concerned as to who would be held responsible for the normal wear and tear in the building? Would it be the day school or the Sunday school?

Conflict began to grow in the midst of a brand new building. The irony of this is astounding. For years, the church worshiped and conducted ministries in an old, antiquated building. In the midst of the building's inadequacy, there was harmony and understanding among the people. However, soon after relocating to a brand new facility, disharmony became commonplace. Where the new building was designed to solve old ministry problems, it became a vehicle for new relational problems.

Also contributing to the growing discontent between the school and the church was the leadership style of the school administrator. He sought to regulate everything pertaining to the school and gave many people the impression that the church was to be subservient to the school. Church board meetings became opportunities for him to request more and more be done for the school: the developing of a playground, a new church sign erected with the school's name prominently displayed, among other items.

Additionally, whenever anyone questioned him about school finances or dress code or suggested a different way of doing things, he became defensive and attempted to manipulate other initially disinterested people into supporting his point of view. As this pattern of behavior continued, tensions in the church began to grow. Perhaps this part of the conflict could be best explained from Proverbs: "A greedy man stirs up strife, but the one who trusts in the Lord will be enriched" (Proverbs 28:25, ESV).

One person with whom the school administrator continued to have conflict with over these matters was the school board chairperson at the time: John's wife. Jennifer became convinced that these actions by the school administrator were wrong and were not God honoring. She addressed her concerns to the school administrator repeatedly. As the situation deteriorated, Jennifer decided to resign from the school board. Her conviction at the time was that this would eliminate possible accusations of collusion between herself and John against the school administrator and decrease the ongoing conflict.

However, rather than defusing the situation Jennifer's resignation accelerated the conflict. This growing animosity soon resulted in what would become a recurring pattern: an accusatory letter against John and Jennifer. The first letter came from the school administrator. He blamed both of them for all the problems he said existed in the church. He called them a "cancer to the congregation." John brought the letter to the attention of the chairman of the elders, who then informed the elder board.

The elders did not agree with the letter and pledged their support for John and Jennifer. Two elders then met with the administrator and attempted to counterpoint his accusations. He was unrepentant and insistent that he was right, the elders were wrong, and that John needed to be fired. The meeting resulted in an impasse.

Jennifer approached the administrator later that week. Speaking to him in the church foyer before the beginning of school, with many people mingling about, Jennifer attempted to reconcile any differences the two of them may have had. She explained that as his sister in Christ, they could disagree on issues, but she did not want them to be disagreeable with each other. Jennifer shook his hand and ended the conversation. It looked to be a good resolution. Jennifer could not have been more mistaken. The academy administrator accused her of making improper, sexual advances toward him when she shook his hand in the foyer. John and Jennifer were shocked. It seemed everything they attempted to do to resolve the conflict was creating more conflict.

John, in cooperation with the chairperson of the elder board, sensed God leading him to address the congregation regarding the issues raised in the letter. The next Sunday morning, John apologized to the church *if* in any way he or his wife had offended anyone. The response from the congregation was tremendous. There was an outpouring of love and support from a vast majority of people. However, the administrator took issue with John's usage of the word "if." In his mind, there was no question that John had offended people and his unwillingness to admit this was sin. The impasse became more intense.

Shortly thereafter, John received a second letter. It was from a church elder, a good friend, and the husband of the church nursery ministry director with whom Jennifer had earlier been in conflict. He left, in John's office mailbox, a four-page letter detailing his opinion that Jennifer and John were the source of the conflict existing in the church.

John waited until he returned home from a spring break vacation and met with the elder for lunch. To John's amazement, the elder apologized for what he had written. He said he really did not believe the things he wrote. Later that day, he called Jennifer and apologized to her.

The remaining weeks of the school year proved to be uneventful. Finally, their summer vacation arrived, and John and his family ventured to their friends home in Virginia for some much needed rest and relaxation. Little did they realize that this would be the calm before the storm.

CHAPTER TEN

The Trial's Full Fury

Upon John's first day back in the office following his summer vacation, he received a phone call from the elder chairman requesting a meeting that morning. When the chairman arrived at the church, he proceeded to inform John the school administrator and his wife demanded that the elders fire him. Their reasons were that John no longer held the congregation's confidence to lead them. In truth, John believed he no longer held this couple's.

Later that week, the entire elder board met with John and Jennifer, the administrator and his wife, and the church nursery director. The question was asked by one of the elders: "Do you want to be right, or do you want to be reconciled?" Everyone pledged their desire to be reconciled. A second question was then asked: "Are you willing to do whatever the elder board asks?" To her credit, Jennifer would not unilaterally agree if it meant compromising biblical principles. The meeting was brief, and everyone expressed forgiveness and again asked for the same from all involved.

The following week, another meeting was set up for John and Jennifer to meet with an elder and his wife for the purpose of detailing all of the issues that existed between them and the school administrator. Now, this is critical. John would not comply with this request. Since he and his wife had forgiven the administrator, and vice versa, they could neither see the value nor the biblical directive (1 Corinthians 13:4–6, ESV) of reviewing, with a third party, what was forgiven.

Was this the right course of action? To this day, John believes it was. He saw the elder's request as adding fuel to an already spreading fire. He did not provide the elder with an itemized list of grievances, and the elder was not pleased. He accused John and Jennifer of being unsubmissive to his authority and Jennifer unsubmissive to John's. The meeting cnded acrimoniously.

The following week, the elders met and placed John on a mandated sabbatical. This was in lieu of an earlier meeting that week wherein John reiterated his refusal to comply with providing a list of grievances against the administrator. John had forgiven him, and he did not believe recounting these issues would be profitable or biblical.

The elders' reasons for giving John the sabbatical were as follows: disharmony within the church for which the elders believed John's wife and he were the cause, Jennifer's apparent lack of submissiveness to John as her husband, their apparent need (in one elder's opinion) for marital counseling, and Jennifer's deep (again in one elder's opinion) psychological problems that called for professional counseling. However, what was initially emotionally devastating to the two of them became the beginning of a heavenly healing process which was abundant, sweet, and a time of unprecedented spiritual growth for their family. John and Jennifer gradually began to learn the truth of James 1:1–4 (ESV)

John is a self-confessed workaholic. He loves working in his office, preparing messages, filling his datebook with appointments, setting goals, and making plans. He enjoys visiting the sick and preaching and teaching the word of God. He echoes D. Martin Lloyd-Jones's statement that "preaching is the highest and the greatest and the most glorious calling to which anyone can ever be called" (Lloyd-Jones, 9). All of a sudden, those things were gone. The church elders decreed that he was no longer fit to preach, teach, perform weddings, funerals, or conduct any other ministerial responsibilities as pastor of the church until his family situation, in particular his wife, was fixed. John would remain on salary and was required to attend, with his family, weekly counseling sessions with a mutually agreed upon counselor. Suddenly, John was out of his office, out of ministry, and at home.

Upon hearing the news, the congregation's reaction was widespread confusion about the situation, anger toward the elders, and sympathy for John and Jennifer. People immediately called them pledging their support. Cards flooded their mailbox each day, offering words of encouragement. Many others respected their desire for privacy. A few close friends came to their house to sit and cry with them. John's secretary and her husband were a blessing to his entire family. However, with the notable exception of two elders who called to validate their decision, no one from the elder board communicated with them.

CHAPTER ELEVEN

Joy in the Trial

There were several things John's family and he committed to do during this time in addition to counseling. These included attending a large church in another community where they could anonymously worship, attack the "honey do" list of odd jobs to be done around the house, fulfill the pre-course requirements of his inaugural Doctor of Ministry class at a local seminary, and not initiate any conversation with anyone from the church. If rumors spread and gossip arose, they would not originate with them. When people called, he or Jennifer answered their questions as succinctly as they could but gave no opinion and vented no anger.

It was at this time that God brought numerous blessings into their lives from some unexpected sources. These included:

- A counselor from a nationally known radio program. He was part of this organization's pastoral care line. He listened to John and offered words of encouragement on several occasions.
- The counselors and staff from the counseling ministry retreat John and Jennifer attended. They listened, counseled, challenged, and protected John and Jennifer with integrity and grace. The retreat, which was a renewal

center for pastors, missionaries, Christian workers, and their families, provided wonderful counsel and encouragement for John's family. During their sabbatical, John and Jennifer attended weekly counseling sessions and then spent three weeks there on retreat where they were able to honestly examine their hurts, address their anger at the circumstances, forgive those who were attacking them, and proactively pray concerning their hopeful return to ministry. They met several other couples who also were damaged in their ministries and through a twenty-one-day bonding period they came away with lifelong, caring comrades. Their counselor determined that Jennifer was a submissive wife and did not have deep psychological problems.

- The surprising opportunity for John to teach at a local university. This part-time position gave him an avenue to channel his energy and to be useful outside of the home.
- The administration at the local seminary, which encouraged John when the conflict was as its peak. These were busy men with numerous responsibilities, but they took a personal interest in John. They let him know that he was of value and still useful to the Lord.
- The church, John and his family benefited firsthand from an evangelistic association that provided biblical mediation. Their representative provided professional and biblical intervention that proved to be calm in the midst of the storm, which promoted healing throughout the church. John thoroughly appreciated his clear objectivity and his consistent professionalism. On top of all that, the mediator was a great encourager and an eager listener. While he may have appeared detached on the outside, as he needed to be, he truly cared for John's

> family and everyone's personal and ministerial well-being. He conducted church wide interviews concerning John's ministry. His conclusion, which he shared with John and Jennifer following their interview with him, was that there was no reason why John should have been removed from the pulpit.

Through all of these avenues, God brought healing to John's family and him. However, the conflict at the church intensified. Many people observed that even though Jennifer was accused of causing and contributing to the conflict, rather than abating during their four-month departure, the church conflict grew worse. The school administrator, who had verbally attacked John and his family, now attacked the elders who had previously supported him. He became an individual seemingly out of control as the elders passively watched. What irony! Jennifer and John now believe that God withdrew them from the situation at the church in order for the leadership to see who, indeed, was responsible for creating the conflict within the church.

At the end of the summer and at the conclusion of their three-week retreat at the counseling center, the church's elder chairman called and left a message on John's answering machine. He wanted to meet with John and Jennifer. John returned his call and confirmed a meeting time for that evening. John's two daughters anguished that their father was going to be fired from his job. When the gentleman arrived, he asked them how they were doing and how their family was. When John told him his daughters were downstairs crying, fearing their dad was going to lose his job, the elder broke down in tears.

He presented a letter signed by him and another elder, indicating the elder board's decision to welcome John back to full-time ministry at the church. The proposed return date was slated for the beginning of the New Year. This elder, Jennifer, and John had a precious time of reconciliation and forgiveness as he expressed his sorrow and grief regarding all that happened to them, and how sinful, selfish people had been allowed to control the church. They felt vindicated, but they also knew a difficult road lay ahead.

The mediator conducted reconciliation meetings John and Jennifer had with the elders and anyone within the church who requested such. The only ones who met with them were some individual elders, along with their wives, with each meeting resulting in forgiveness, understanding, and reconciliation.

Following the meetings, the mediator commended Jennifer and John for their willingness to submit to the mediation process. He knew it had been a hard four months for their family, but he also stated God was being glorified through them. This was a wonderful statement of affirmation.

Their first Sunday back worshiping at the church, they arrived late and sat off to the side of the center aisle. John did not preach. When the service ended, many within the congregation greeted them with much love and affection. John returned to the pulpit the following Sunday. While it was difficult to return, after all which had occurred, John and his family knew this was what God wanted.

Following the mediator's counsel, the elder board requested the school administrator meet with them. He refused to do so. After repeated attempts to initiate a meeting and his continued refusal to comply, the elders had no choice but to terminate his employment.

He did not take his firing well and sent an inflammatory letter, against the elders, to the parents of the school's students. Several congregational meetings followed wherein the elders endeavored to explain their decision and answer parents' questions. It was a difficult and emotional time for all involved. However, God eventually brought peace.

One of the newly appointed elders became interim school administrator for the balance of the school year and did an admirable job. He not only managed the school's financial affairs well but also established harmony between the teachers, parents of students, and the church leadership. The worst was finally over.

CHAPTER TWELVE

The Aftermath of the Trial

I can identify with John. Perhaps it is also reminiscent of your stormy conflict. God teaches many lessons through trials. Some of them are difficult to learn. In addition, principles that God teaches leaders in past experiences He teaches again for the leader's renewal and recommitment to Him. While painful, trials prove to be profitable for the leader and his family to become more like Christ. God uses conflict to further develop you and me into becoming a more refined godly and joyful leader.

Joy is not dependent upon, nor derived from, outward circumstances but rather from an inner tranquility of one's soul anchored to the gospel of Jesus Christ. Regardless of the situation and circumstances, the peaceful calm of a joyful spirit, produced by the Holy Spirit, transcends any conflict.

Through trials I have encountered, I came to know God more fully by developing a greater sense of joyful contentment in Him. Along with my family, He is all I have. Preaching, teaching, counseling, and assorted other ministerial duties can be taken away. Yet when a leader cannot minister to others, God ministers to him and fosters contentment in Him alone. God accomplishes this through His word and through prayer.

As J. I. Packer writes, "Those who know God have great contentment in God. There is no peace like the peace of those whose minds are possessed with full assurance that they have known God, and God has known them, and that this relationship guarantees God's favor to them in life, through death and on forever" (Packer, 31).

Even though God called me into the ministry, the ministry alone must not be the sum total of one's righteous standing in Him. Even though I serve God in a full-time church related vocation, the ministry cannot become a substitute for God. I often wonder if I at times have been more in love with the ministry than with the Lord and He allowed the ministry to be taken away to show me where my priorities need to be. The ministry, in whatever form or function, is a poor substitute for the Lord.

Conflict is inevitable. It is inevitable in government, business, families, and in the local church. The scores of biblical passages on church conflict testify to this reality. As a pastor, I desired to avoid conflict as much as possible and to be accommodating to everyone. However, I learned that conflict must not be avoided but rather confronted. Only then can it truly be managed.

Conflict originates with worldliness (1 John 2:15–17, ESV), fleshly desires (James 4:1–2, ESV), and the devil (1 Peter 5:1–9, ESV; Ephesians 4:25–27, 6:11–12, ESV). Motivations, personal leadership styles, and the thirst for power may become avenues in which the world, the flesh, and the devil may seek to begin a conflict. The truth of James 3:13–18 (ESV) resonates here when it says:

> Who is wise and understanding among you? Let him show by good conduct that his works are done in the meekness of wisdom. But if you have bitter envy and self-seeking in your hearts, do not boast and lie against the truth. This wisdom does not descend from above, but is

> earthly, sensual, and demonic. For where envy and self-seeking exist, confusion and every evil thing are there. But the wisdom that is from above is first pure, then peaceable, gentle, willing to yield, full of mercy and good fruits, without partiality and without hypocrisy. Now the fruit of righteousness is sown in peace by those who make peace.

There may be times when a leader, his family, along with others in the church or organization, bears the brunt of an individual's bitter envy, self-seeking, and boasting. Initially, the leader may merely be frustrated by the resulting confusion and perplexity of being unable to solve the conflicts around him. The leader may not understand why people cannot see what he witnesses in those who were causing problems. James 3:13–18 (ESV) gives leaders the biblical instruction to finally understand the magnitude, scope, and source of the turmoil.

First, the wisdom conveyed by human initiators of conflict is "earthly" meaning "weak and perishable" (Kittel, 117). "Its derogatory sense is obvious in Philippians 3:19 where Paul says that the enemies of the cross of Christ have their minds set on earthly things" (Moo, 134).

Second, this wisdom is unspiritual, sensual, and does not originate with God but rather with human feelings and reason. People feel justified in their actions because their motivations for those actions are not sourced in God but rather in their own emotions and human logic. They become determined to achieve their goals by whatever means necessary, even if this means slandering those who disagree with them.

Third, this wisdom is demonic. Perhaps it is demonic in nature and character, as well as devilish in origin. God illuminated the meaning of this verse to me, and I understand that I do not fight an earthly battle but rather a spiritual battle.

The church can become demonized, and people within the church become the instruments of this attack. No other explanation makes sense. The blindness by many to sinful behavior is a spiritual blindness caused by the devil through his demons. This time period will be the most intense spiritual battle the leader will ever encounter. Spiritual warfare no longer is just a theological doctrine but rather an ongoing, intense, and present reality within the limits of God's sovereignty.

A pastor must continually communicate with his flock and elder board. Letters, newsletters, e-mails, and conversations with people in the proper setting are all valuable tools to keep conflict at bay. The more one communicates, the possibility of misunderstanding and rumor is lessened.

It is important to distinguish the different responses people display when encountering conflict. They may run from it, they may attack it, or they may seek a reasonable solution for it. I habitually ran from and avoided conflict as much as I could. I no longer do. I address it, confront it, and seek a biblical solution for it.

Each leader is personally responsible for their leadership development. Whether it as a pastor, business owner, physician, attorney, or elected official. When conflict arises, and it will, a godly leader must pray for God's perspective. He or she must become accountable to mentors and other leaders within the church or organization. They must learn to feed on God's word and other resources enabling them to remain positive. They must seek prayer support and contact leaders outside the organization who have successfully navigated through similar conflict. It is within these disciplines that they remain strong in Christ.

One of the easiest things to do as a leader in conflict—look for another job—is one of the most foolish things to do. Each church or organization has the same assortment of difficult people: the old guard, the strong-willed, the embittered, the hiders, the demonized, the gossipers, the know-it-alls, the prideful, and the hateful. The names and the faces may be different, but the issues will be the same. I have decided it is much wiser to shepherd the people I already know than go to another church and have to become acquainted with a whole new set of problems and problem people. The same is true for any leader. The grass is never greener somewhere else.

Conflict in the church, and particularly at the church board level, may stem from personality differences, and clashes with those differences, as opposed to sin. People tend to view life, and issues of life, from their own personal orientation toward life. Placing a group of people into leadership responsibilities who are unaware of their inherent differences and similarities is a recipe for conflict.

When my wife and I attended a three-week retreat, we studied a program called Life Orientation Training or LIFO. Dr. Stuart Atkins, a behavioral scientist and organizational consultant, developed this program enabling organizations to be more productive in their work and more influential when dealing with key people. While not a Christian based program, it is a curriculum assisting in the discovery of an individual's leadership traits, strengths, and weaknesses, thereby fostering an understanding of one's own leadership style and how this interacts with someone else's.

The program's breakdown of four major personality traits was reminiscent of Dr. Tim LaHaye's material in his book *Spirit-Controlled Temperament*. Participants in LIFO answer questions regarding their reactions to favorable and unfavorable life situations. Their responses to these situations reveal their predominant personality traits. The four personality types are:

- The people pleaser. These are people who seek to please other people, no matter the cost. For them, no sacrifice is too great or service to small. They are emotionally orientated, and they desire harmony above all else.
- The conservative. This is the individual who wants to go slow and be sure. They will check and double-check their facts and figures before they make a decision—that is, if they make a decision. They may decide that the most responsible thing to do is nothing while accumulating more facts and figures.
- The perfectionist. This is the individual who is concerned with the pursuit of excellence. They are principled and cooperative. Their motto is "If something is to be done, it should be done in excellence or not at all."
- The controller. This is the individual who wants to be in charge. Regardless of title, they are persistent, initiating, urgent, and directing.

The board of directors at the church I pastor contains combinations of all four personality types. What I found interesting is that people are usually not one specific trait but rather a combination of two of more. In addition, a person's predominant personality trait may vary in different situations and circumstances depending on whether a situation is a positive or a negative one.

A year after a particular church conflict, our church board spent a weekend going through the LIFO program. It proved to be a profitable time in revealing our strengths and weaknesses as a board. Our leadership team came away with a greater understanding of why board members act the way they do in certain circumstances and how this can work to the church's advantage and for God's glory.

Leadership is relational and not merely positional. The nurturing of relationships will strengthen a leader's position, while damaging relationships will surely cause a leader to suffer. My family and I came through this trial, and I eventually returned to the church as pastor, not only because it was God's will but also because of the strong, encouraging relationships God gave us within the church.

Throughout conflict, it is imperative to learn to lean on the sufficiency of God's grace. Leaders many times battle with pride and self-sufficiency. The leader knows it. So does God. A major reason God brings conflict into a godly leader's life is to eliminate the idol of self and replace it with a proper focus and dependence upon God and His grace. God humbled me in order to use me for His glory.

The Lord told Paul, "My grace is sufficient for you" (2 Corinthians 12:9, ESV). In this passage, grace means "God's divine assistance to us [believers] through the Holy Spirit" (Bridges, 137). John Calvin wrote that "here the word grace does not mean as elsewhere God's favour, but is used by metonymy [to indicate] the help of the Holy Spirit, which comes to us from God's undeserved favour" (Calvin, 161). Jerry Bridges wisely states:

> God never allows pain without a purpose in the lives of His children. He never allows Satan, not circumstances, not any ill-intending person to afflict us unless He uses that affliction for our good. God never wastes pain. He always causes it to work together for our ultimate good, the good of conforming us more to the likeness of His Son. (Bridges, 139)

Finally, there is the truth of Romans 8:28 (NASB): "And we know that [God causes] all things to work together for good to those who love God, to those who are the called according to *His* purpose" (Romans 8:28, ESV). God is the active cause of all things working together for good. This promise is not for everyone but only for the one who loves God—that is, those who are called or invited to salvation thereby becoming a child of God. God is sovereign, and in His providence, He orchestrates every event in life, including conflicts. The purpose of such is to accomplish God's purpose. "Many of the things comprised are evil in themselves and it is the marvel of God's wisdom and grace that they, when taken in concert with the whole, are made to work for good" (Murray, 314).

"God has a great and eternal plan for mankind and for each person on earth. So despite human sinfulness, and even in the midst of it, God works out His glorious redemptive intentions in the lives of those who look to Him and trust Him" (Narramore, 10).

The present situation at the church I serve is what I refer to as smoldering embers. Many good things are happening, but conflict continues to rear its ugly head from time to time. However, I am now better able to handle the conflicts because of the refining fire God brought me through and the strength He provides by His Spirit through His word.

Several families have left the church. Some left out of conviction against the elder's decision to fire the school administrator, whereas others left out of loyalty to those who had those convictions. Some who left have now returned. Others who left will probably never return.

The congregation is slowly learning to trust the elder board again, as am I. It has not been easy, and it is hard to forget the many words spoken against my wife and me along with the then seemingly self-righteous demeanor of the church's spiritual leaders. I am presently reticent to share many personal thoughts with the elder board regarding what is going on in my life. The old adage "once burned, twice shy" applies here, I guess. I am concerned that what I may share could be used against me as in the past. One author has written, "Renewal is often painful" (Barrs, 9). However, God is helping me through this issue. The healing process, while slow, is progressing.

My wife continues to heal. God is faithful, and I am grateful. She has taught a Sunday school class, and she presently sings with me in a Sunday morning worship team. As of this writing, we have also taught a Sunday school class on parenting.

The school has closed. Rising unemployment and a downturned economy resulted in a significant lack of enrollment. Prior to its closing, the ministry was being accepted as an integral part of the church.

My prayer is that those who join me in serving the Lord as a pastor will benefit from what we and the church went through and what God taught us. The Apostle Paul states:

> Blessed be the God and Father of our Lord Jesus Christ, the Father of mercies and God of all comfort, who comforts us in all our tribulation, that we may be able to comfort those who are in any trouble, with the comfort with which we ourselves are comforted by God. For as the sufferings of Christ abound in us, so our consolation also abounds through Christ. Now if we are afflicted, it is for your consolation and salvation, which is effective for enduring the same sufferings which we also suffer. Or if we are comforted, it is for your consolation and salvation. And our hope for you is steadfast, because we know that as you are partakers of the sufferings, so also you will partake of the consolation. (2 Corinthians 1:3–7, ESV)

My desire is that I can embody the principles found in 2 Corinthians 1:3–7 (ESV) by being a Christ appointed comforter to those in the ministry needing comfort from the God of all comfort. I also hope that when the next conflict comes, and it will, I will instinctively "count it all joy." I do not pretend to possess all the answers to conflict or godly leadership. I simply know what I learned from God through conflict and how I am a better pastor, husband, father, friend, and godly leader.

CHAPTER THIRTEEN

Pastors' Responses to Conflict Survey

I believe this ministry of comfort has already begun as a result of this book. If I did not realize it before, I am not the only pastor or leader who has encountered God ordained conflict. Many of my friends and fellow pastors have experienced their own firestorms.

This realization prompted me to compile a series of questions pertaining to the issue of God directed conflict in developing godly leadership. The ten questions I formulated arose from the particular circumstances I encountered in my own trial. I wondered if other pastors had learned as much about leadership as I had from the conflicts they encountered. I submitted these questions to colleagues of mine.

I was overwhelmed by the responses I received. Each one who responded to my letter spoke of a difficult time of conflict he had encountered, or was presently encountering, in leadership. The respondents shared what God had taught them or was presently teaching them through their experiences. Each related how his circumstances deeply affected them and made him a better leader. However, one response was particularly poignant:

Dear Tom,

> I started to fill out this survey and I could feel my stomach and chest tightening in the same way that they did when we went through our church split that ended in the closing of the doors of our two year old church plant. And, to be honest with you, as I tried to answer some of the initial questions in your survey, I was made painfully aware that I still have a root of bitterness in my person that would come out in my answers to you. So, now that I have made a confession to you, I hope you will forgive me for not participating in your survey.

I responded to my friend and assured him that I would pray for him and that there was no need for me to forgive him for not participating in the survey. I expressed to him my appreciation for his candor. However, his response does bring to light the issue that recovering from ministerial conflict, and seeing God's purpose in it, happens neither quickly nor automatically. The leadership qualities acquired through God ordained conflict may take the leader months to acknowledge and even longer to appreciate. Meanwhile, the flood of emotions resulting from conflict's deep hurts may linger and adversely affect the wounded leader. I can identify with his anguish and understand his bitterness, but I also know that great good can result from the great pain the leader encounters in serving Christ. I am glad God brought me to this perspective. I am confident He will do the same with my friend.

The survey questions I posed, and their respective responses, are as follows.

Question one: When have you recently encountered conflict in your pastoral ministry? Briefly describe the circumstances surrounding the conflict.

All respondents indicated a conflict they had experienced or were presently experiencing. The issues involved included:

- poor staff relationships,
- inappropriate sexual behavior by a colleague with a woman in the church,
- church officers' demands for the pastor's resignation because of his failure to preach solely evangelistic messages,
- a church board member's attempts for a hostile takeover of the leadership of the church resulting in his eventual removal from leadership,
- church members being angry about an auction scheduled to take place in the church,
- disagreements over the vision of the church and how to implement it, and
- an individual not permitted to give a public testimony due to the person's inconsistent Christian character.

Question two: Did the church conflict ever stem from any unspoken expectations (tacit norms) the congregation had pertaining to you, your wife, or your children? If so, what were those expectations?

Two-thirds of those responding indicated that they experienced unspoken expectations in their pastorate, and their failure to meet those "tacit norms" were in part the reason for their conflict. One respondent explained that he immediately succeeded a pastor who had been at the church for thirty-seven years. "They expected me to do things the way the previous pastor had done, or at least allow the congregation to carry on as they had done for years. I did not meet those expectations, which created the conflict."

Question three: How did you respond to the church conflict? Was there any accommodation on your part? Did you pretend everything was okay? Did you ignore the situation? Did you resign and leave the church? Did you display anger, and if so, at whom? Was there any confrontation or church discipline?

The responses and results varied. One pastor at first ignored the conflict, knowing that he was right and the congregation would see it. However, when the problem did not dissipate, he publicly confronted the individual in question. Another pastor immediately confronted the conflict but ultimately resigned his pastorate when the unhealthiness of the situation began to affect his family on many levels.

One respondent indicated that he became angry, whereas another confronted his elder board about its failure to protect the congregation from the conflict. Still another indicated that he confronted the individual in question immediately because the conflict was recognized by everyone involved as a work of Satan, and it could not continue. Finally, one pastor indicated he responded with a mixture of anger, confrontation, and fear.

Question four: What positive benefits, if any, did the church conflict have for you and your family? What were the negatives?

All respondents spoke of both positive and negative outcomes. The benefits from conflict included:

- having a new vision for church ministry,
- having personal growth by dealing with jealousy and pride along with a greater trust in God,
- taking charge of the hiring of church staff,
- having a greater involvement in administration,
- leading the elder board with greater vision and direction,
- acquiring a spiritual toughness along with a learned humility,

- standing by convictions,
- becoming closer to one's wife,
- developing a greater prioritization of responsibilities,
- honing listening and counseling skills,
- establishing family boundaries that the church congregation may not trespass,
- praying and trusting God more than before,
- In jest, one pastor indicated that a positive benefit to church conflict he encountered was that he was now a firm believer in capital punishment.

The negative results due to conflict included:

- people leaving the church,
- personal anxiousness and stress related health issues,
- congregational hypocrisy,
- spouses pulling back from ministry and social involvement,
- negative publicity in the community concerning the church and the pastor,
- people seeking to instigate further conflict with the pastor,
- time and energy which could have been used for more productive matters,
- struggling with forgiveness,
- the negative impact on the pastor's children and family,
- loss of close friendships,
- sleeplessness,
- grinding teeth at night,
- thinking way too much about the situation, which distracted from spiritual growth, and
- physical exhaustion.

One pastor wrote that "the full force of this event broke right at the time that my wife and I left for our twenty-fifth wedding anniversary to Hawaii. I was personally wiped out and I was not sure that I would even have a church to attend when I returned. In hindsight, it was the right thing to do because physical restoration for me personally started during that trip."

Question five: What would you do differently in facing another church conflict? What would you do similarly?

In handling the conflict differently, all who responded indicated they would address any conflict sooner in future situations as opposed to hoping it would just go away. Most indicated a desire to share more with the church leadership instead of keeping the conflict between the individuals involved. One pastor would involve a third party immediately and confront more quickly with love. Seeking advice from many counselors was suggested.

One respondent indicated that he would not allow an elder board to keep any conflict secret from the congregation, he would document his thoughts in writing and not allow the subordinate staff to ignore his reprimands and teaching. Another pastor indicated that he should have shared more clearly his philosophy of ministry to the church leadership. Following the principles of church discipline from Matthew 18 more quickly was also suggested. One pastor wrote:

> I think a lot about what I would have done differently. I have had several situations here at the church as we transitioned from one pastor to the other that caused conflict. In each situation, I wonder if I had to do it over again, would I do it differently. I think the answer is yes. Since I do not like conflict, when it comes I let it go for awhile but sooner or later I must deal with it. I do not

> always deal with it correctly. I would try to communicate with that person more openly. I might have to use a third party to help us get together. I would try to give that person more grace.

In what they would do the same, one pastor wrote that he would talk with people regardless of their stance on the issue. Others indicated they would do the following:

- continue to seek reconciliation privately and consult an outside mediator to work with the church leadership and the pastor,
- continue to oppose any behavior that hurts people or puts programs above people,
- be open, honest, and public with the issues that the congregation faces, and
- confront individuals as necessary.

Confronting conflict, and doing it quickly, seemed to be the underlying theme by all respondents. They recognized that running away from conflict acerbates the situation and is not good leadership because eventually you have to confront the difficulty. The perspective is to confront—the sooner, the better.

Question six: Did you have any support system in place, besides God and the Bible, to help you through the church conflict: such as, counselors, friends, coworkers, or colleagues in ministry?

Many listed pastoral friends, leadership in the church, a professional counselor, professors and students in seminaries they attended, friends, accountability groups, ministry colleagues, along with wife and family. Only one pastor indicated he did not have any outside support system at the time of his conflict.

However, he now has a leadership group in place that assists him in discussing and handling difficult situations as they arise.

Question seven: What caused you the most frustration during the church conflict? What steps do you think could have been taken, by you or others, to avoid and/ or reduce the intensity of the conflict?

What caused the most frustration for these pastors included:

- not being able to defend themselves against false reports,
- choosing to take one's lumps and stay on the "high road" by not engaging in arguments,
- lack of communication,
- not being able to "fix" the situation,
- not being as sensitive and proactive as necessary,
- watching people act so poorly toward each other,
- people not realizing the consequences of their words and behavior,
- the church officers not acting in a wise or spiritual manner in the way they approached the situation,
- the church splitting and people leaving,
- people choosing to gossip,
- when the conflict involved facts that were not clear thus making it hard to address,
- not being able to include friends within the church for support,
- unfounded charges, and
- a lack of support from the elder board.

One pastor stated:

> The lack of support from the elder board caused the most frustration. I had been at the church for twenty years and

faithfully served this church. My whole adult life was given to this church. It hurt that the guys who knew my integrity would think that I would do what I was doing due to petty differences with the youth minister. Also, I was frustrated by the elders having secret meetings. I was then, and am now, an elder of this church and there should have been no meetings without my knowledge or participation.

Question eight: What was the greatest blessing you received during, and after, the church conflict? Were there any blessings?

Each respondent indicated that, indeed, blessings did occur in the aftermath of their firestorm. These included:

- affirmation and support from the congregation,
- support from the board chairman,
- a greater closeness to one's wife,
- an improved walk with God,
- the church having a greater zeal for God,
- people assuming leadership roles which had not occurred previously,
- experiencing God's faithfulness, and
- considering God's principles regarding conflict.

Others mentioned:

- moving to Florida and leaving the unhealthiness behind,
- possessing parameters for protecting one's heart and home when it came to the unhealthy behavior of unhealthy people,
- knowing where to stand on conflict,
- being forced to look deeper into Scripture and evaluate one's theology,

- experiencing spiritual growth in a way that would have never happened otherwise,
- seeing a new vision for the church,
- loosing innocence, and
- God working all things to His glory, including changing one's attitude.

Question nine: How did the church conflict affect your relationships with the individuals involved? Did they leave the church? Did you? Are you close to them? Do you speak to them? Do you socialize with them? Did you forgive them? Did they forgive you? Do you trust them or are you emotionally guarded whenever you are around them?

Many indicated the people they were in conflict with did leave the church. Most shared that they remain guarded, cautious, and are having a hard time trusting people. Several received letters requesting forgiveness, whereas others indicated they are careful in what they say for fear of giving people information to use against them.

One individual wrote that he does not trust the church's officers, and another indicated he has acquired a great relationship with the staff persons who were involved in conflict with him. However, he writes that while "I enjoy our times together and feel no pain concerning the conflict years ago, it did take three years of working through the issues to get to this point. I fully trust both of these two men."

One pastor responded that the conflict affected his relationship with the parties involved very detrimentally, that they did not leave the church, that he is not close to them, and does not have much social contact with them. He is intentionally trying to rebuild trust, but he admits that he is very guarded and distrusting of them.

Another respondent indicated that he has asked for forgiveness on three separate occasions but has never received either an acknowledgement of such or an apology in return. He does not trust the people who were involved in the conflict.

Others indicated that the youth pastor left, along with six of the church elders. Of the six, one has met with the pastor and apologized but has not returned to the church. There are doubts that the church would accept him.

Finally, these are the thoughts of a pastor in Florida who responds:

> Some people walked away from us and the church because of their unhealthiness and their callous attitude. We have maintained cordial friendships with others, but while we act politely we are keeping our distance. Some relationships deepened and became stronger because of this refining process. Many people left the church and found healthy churches to attend and received healing. My family does not socialize with many people from that period of conflict because of our subsequent move to Florida. One summer, we found ourselves around some of the participants from the ordeal at a wedding I officiated. I was open and honest with all of them in regards to the new direction my family had been placed in and offered answers when asked about coming back to the Cincinnati area (which was no because of our commitment to Florida). I have come back to the understanding of grace and mercy and I am able to be real with people again, especially when the conversation finds itself about the implosion of the church. I am now able to be honest and true with my words, not verbally attack people, but rather encourage them to see what God

is doing in their world today. Have I forgiven and moved on? Yes!

Question ten: What primary lesson did God teach you throughout your ordeal? What does He continue to teach you regarding conflict?

One pastor said to stay in Florida whereas another added the biggest lesson he learned was to leave the pastorate and become a milkman. Seriously, many spoke of:

- reinforced patience,
- a more fervent prayer life,
- friendships need to be grounded in honesty, accountability, vulnerability, and open communication,
- taking seriously the responsibility to lead,
- to institute accountability within the church for both paid and unpaid staff, and
- that in this world, there will be tribulation and living to prevent it is not a realistic possibility.

One pastor stressed the importance of trust, personal integrity, and a commitment to build relationships. Others indicated the need to address conflict quickly and build relationships at every opportunity.

One respondent indicated that God taught him that time is a great healer, if a person will forgive. He added, "God has shown me that life is too short to allow conflict to destroy. I am continually learning that conflict will always exist in ministry; effective pastors must learn how to handle it personally and how to manage it within the church."

Additional lessons learned included:

- to be personally and spiritually prepared for life and ministry that will involve conflict,
- to maintain physical health as much as possible by exercise and a correct diet,
- to give attention to the spiritual disciplines of prayer, Scripture reading, meditation, and memorization, and
- to be prepared for the unexpected.

Another lesson was firmness to one's biblical convictions. One pastor responded:

> Even though you minister grace and mercy from the Almighty weekly, there are times that a firm stance is required that is biblical, honest, and that keeps in mind the message of restoration. This is not about judging, but rather about firm leadership in the context of mercy and restoration. Firmness is required.

Additionally, others stated that there is the need for Christ's daily provision and strength, the need to communicate with people, to set a righteous example, to be willing to listen, and to recognize that the church belongs to God. What resonates with pastors currently concerning the issue of God developing leaders through conflict was an important sympathy with pastors in history. As Jonathan Edwards stated following his dismissal from the pastorate at Northampton First Church:

> God tries the graces of his people by persecutions that the truth and power of his grace in them may appear to his own glory, both before men, angels, and devils. Our end is that by such discovery of the truth and strength of their faith and love, he may as it were triumph over Satan; and

make him to see what a victory is obtained over him, by so rescuing those souls that were once his captives from his power; and convince him of the real success of his design of redeeming and sanctifying souls. (Murray, 352)

CHAPTER FOURTEEN

Implementing Strategies and Goals

What practical value does writing this book provide for me, fellow pastors, leaders, and the church? There must be some practical and ongoing profit in acknowledging that conflict is an indispensable element that God uses to develop godly leaders. I believe there is.

This text is a memorial to God's purpose and His sovereignty. God taught me much regarding pastoral leadership through the conflict I encountered and this book records and recognizes those lessons for my remembrance, for God's glory, and I trust, for the benefit of present and future leaders. I believe it may parallel another memorial God instructed His children to erect.

When the children of Israel crossed the Jordan River following forty years of wilderness wanderings (Joshua 3) the Lord then spoke to Joshua saying:

> When all the nation had finished passing over the Jordan, the Lord said to Joshua, "Take twelve men from the people, from each tribe a man, and command them, saying, 'Take twelve stones from here out of the midst of the Jordan, from the very place where the priests' feet stood firmly, and bring them over with you and lay them

> down in the place where you lodge tonight.'" Then Joshua called the twelve men from the people of Israel, whom he had appointed, a man from each tribe. And Joshua said to them, "Pass on before the ark of the Lord your God into the midst of the Jordan, and take up each of you a stone upon his shoulder, according to the number of the tribes of the people of Israel, that this may be a sign among you. When your children ask in time to come, 'What do those stones mean to you?' then you shall tell them that the waters of the Jordan were cut off before the ark of the covenant of the Lord. When it passed over the Jordan, the waters of the Jordan were cut off. So these stones shall be to the people of Israel a memorial forever." (Joshua 4:1–7, ESV)

A sign, from the word תוֹא *(owt),* can mean anything from "a mark, a token, an ensign, a standard, a miracle, a proof, or a warning. In the context of Joshua 4:6, sign means either a warning to the rebellious or it points backward to a historical event" (TWOT, 18–19).

A memorial, from the word ןוֹרָכִּז *(zikarown)* is "a memento, a memorable thing, day, or writing" (TWOT, 242). "It is an object or act which brings something else to mind or which represents something else. As such it may be a memorial, a reminder, a historical record, or a physical token which calls to mind a deity" (242). What is it that God desires Israel to remember about Him? Joshua 4:20–24 (ESV) explains:

> And those twelve stones, which they took out of the Jordan, Joshua set up at Gilgal. And he said to the people of Israel, "When your children ask their fathers in times to come, 'What do these stones mean?' then you shall let

> your children know, 'Israel passed over this Jordan on dry ground.' For the Lord your God dried up the waters of the Jordan for you until you passed over, as the Lord your God did to the Red Sea, which he dried up for us until we passed over, so that all the peoples of the earth may know that the hand of the Lord is mighty, that you may fear the Lord your God forever."

Mighty, from the word חָזָק, *(ḥazaq)* means "strong and powerful" (TWOT, 276). Fear, from the word יָרֵא, *(yarē, yarēʾ)* means "reverence or awe" (TWOT, 399). God wanted the Israelites to set up the memorial as a place to remember God's great strength and to solicit reverence and awe of Him.

This book is not a tribute in any way to my writing abilities, my pastoral ministry, or any leadership skills I may possess. Rather, this book's goal is to glorify God and to edify current leaders in the midst of conflict and to prepare future leaders who will face conflict, with the truth that God is in control and His purposes for their lives are being accomplished.

God's might has not diminished over time nor has the Christian's responsibility to fear and revere Him as the only wise, eternal God. As God instructed Joshua to erect twelve stones as a memorial to Israel of His faithfulness, I believe this book can be the memorial God has directed me to erect. This is especially true when there are few writings addressing the issue of God developing godly leaders though conflict. May this text be "to the praise of His glorious grace" (Ephesians 1:6a).

Leaders in conflict need to know of the many Christian ministries seeking to help the hurting pastor and his family. While I was ignorant of them before the conflict I encountered, God sovereignly directed some wonderful people and ministries into my family's life at a most opportunc time. Pastors presently locked in conflict may glean insights, encouragement, professional mediation, and a comforting ear from organizations committed to the minister, his family, and the local church.

First, Focus on the Family (www.family.org) provides a website link for ministers and their families entitled Thriving Pastor. It can be accessed online at www.thrivingpastor.org. The website contains numerous articles pertaining to family and ministry issues. It also provides pastoral resources to help pastors, their families, and churches care and assist one another.

The Pastoral Care-Giving Ministries link provides numerous categories for pastoral and leadership assistance. These categories include leadership and conflict consultants, financial and legal consultants, reflection and relaxation providers, rest and renewal retreat centers, restoration and counseling retreat centers, psychologists and counseling offices, treatment centers, clinics and hospitals, and numerous miscellaneous ministries.

Additionally, there is a Pastoral Care Line that is available Monday through Friday from 9:00 a.m. to 4:00 p.m. (mountain standard time). A pastor can call toll free, at (877) 233-4455, and speak with someone who will listen, provide a referral, and demonstrate understanding for the hurting. Whereas I have appreciated Focus on the Family in the past because of its philosophy of ministry and the passion of its founder Dr. James Dobson, I am personally indebted to it for its concern for pastors and local churches.

Second, the Ron Susek Evangelistic Association provides a church conflict division to assist churches and pastors encountering conflict. Located in Gettysburg, Pennsylvania, the association is involved in providing evangelistic crusades, spiritual life seminars, and leadership conferences. Ron is the author of *Firestorm*, an informative book addressing how to prevent, recognize, and overcome church conflicts.

The association also provides conflict consultants who endeavor to mediate church conflict when it has reached an impasse. Dr. Ed Peirce, *Director of SEA's church mediation and conflict management division,* is one such individual. He mediated the conflict situation the church encountered, addressed the problem issues to the church leadership and congregation, validated my worth as a pastor and leader, provided tremendous encouragement for my wife in confronting the congregation's unspoken expectations of her, and directed numerous informational and reconciliation meetings. He not only was a professional and valuable consultant, but he also became an encouraging colleague whom I am privileged to know. His courageous leadership will never be forgotten.

Third, is Ken Sande's book, *The Peacemaker*. The author provides insightful information regarding church conflict and the godly leader's biblical way to minister while in the midst of conflict. His evaluation regarding the various ways conflict is addressed, and how it should be addressed, was most valuable.

Fourth, Alongside Inc. is a ministry located in Richland, Michigan, committed to providing professional, spiritual, mental, and emotional caregiving services for individuals and families who are involved in Christian ministry. Alongside is a nonprofit organization that seeks to restore relationships among Christian leaders who are making an impact around the world. They exist to promote personal wholeness and ministry effectiveness in Christian ministry.

Alongside Inc. provides not only weekly counseling opportunities but also monthly three-week retreats offered at the Gull Lake Bible Conference facilities. My wife and I attended one of their retreats that features personal counseling sessions, group meetings, community development with other hurting pastors or missionaries and their spouses, along with worship and fellowship opportunities. For twenty-one days, we resided in a comfortable two-bedroom cottage, where we were able to cook our own meals, read, rest, exercise, recover from the onslaught of conflict, and personally prepare for the future.

The counselors at Alongside Cares can be contacted by phone, at (269) 671-4809, by e-mail at info@alongsidecares.net, or by accessing their website, which is www.alongsidecares.net. They are an instrument of healing in a world filled with spiritual war wherein pastors, missionaries, and Christian workers are often casualties.

I am burdened for pastors, and their families, who have encountered conflict and who still reel from the aftershocks. They need to be nurtured and encouraged in what may appear to be for them the absence of God's blessing. I am also concerned for young men and women who are preparing for the ministry but who perhaps are unaware and unprepared for the eventual conflict they will encounter in serving the Lord. I am burdened for young individuals, and couples, who need to know that conflict will occur, but that God is in control. He can be trusted, and He wants them to learn from the difficulties they will experience so they too will become effective leaders.

One such couple is Timothy and Carrie. They are young, in love with God and each other, and are committed to serving the Lord in a full-time church-related ministry. Presently, Timothy is serving as a youth and worship pastor in Warsaw, Indiana, while Carrie is a public school teacher. They are parents of two young girls. They are both "pastor's kids" and are well aware of the dynamics of conflict in ministry. In fact, they are my son and daughter-in-law.

Neither of them is naive regarding the realities of church and its impact on the minister and his family, but I believe God wants them prepared, and others like them, for the eventuality that God will bring conflict into their ministry in order to refine and purify their commitment to Him. Rather than dread conflict, I pray they will be prayerfully patient when conflict arises and will see it as an opportunity for spiritual growth from God.

Finally, I see this book as a source of help to ministers and churches who have encountered, or who are encountering, conflict. I believe that by educating those in ministry concerning God's purposes for conflict, these individuals will become more effective leaders.

Conflict and trials are the dark sides of greatness. Loneliness is the continuing companion of one who holds great responsibilities. Loneliness often follows a leader in the aftermath of the noisome crowd. My heroes are those who stood tall in the midst of conflict. They serve as an example of the indispensability of conflict in developing godly leadership.

How ironic that the leaders we most admire are those who have endured the greatest pain, sorrow, and difficulty. It is through the crucible of conflict that individuals, such as the sixteenth President of the United States, Abraham Lincoln, ascended the pinnacle of power and influence to become leaders for the ages.

Donald T. Phillips provides a primer on leadership in a small paperback book entitled *Lincoln on Leadership.* He structures the book into four major areas concerning President Lincoln's leadership: people, character, endeavor, and communication. Regarding character, the author cites numerous anecdotes and refers to Lincoln's archival letters which communicate his ideology regarding honesty and integrity, not acting out of vengeance or spite, having the courage to handle unjust criticism, and being a master of paradox.

The information contained in the book's sixth chapter regarding how to handle unjust criticism reveals much about Abraham Lincoln as well as the indispensability of conflict in developing godly leadership. The conflict President Lincoln endured while in office began as soon as he took the oath of office. Not only did conflict originate from the South, but also from within the Union.

The aforementioned ingredients of great and godly leadership, as demonstrated by President Lincoln, seldom appear in the modern, marketing strategy of multimillion dollar companies, conglomerates, or even churches. We want our leaders well scrubbed, smartly dressed, with clear complexions, a full head of hair, and no skeletons in their closets. We do not inquire as to the hardships suffered or lessons learned which thereby solidify a leader's qualification to lead. We often emphasize and gravitate to the superficial rather than the substantial: the surface of a man rather than the depths of a person. How shortsighted.

The Apostle Paul knew this to be true and he knew it well. The truth of leadership developed through conflict would frame his final thoughts. As Paul neared the end of his life, he wrote a final letter to his young protégé, Timothy. His words were passionate, poignant, and personal to his young son in the faith. They would become part of the biblical canon. They are found in 2 Timothy 3:10–15 (ESV) which states:

> You, however, have followed my teaching, my conduct, my aim in life, my faith, my patience, my love, my steadfastness, my persecutions and sufferings that happened to me at Antioch, at Iconium, and at Lystra—which persecutions I endured; yet from them all the Lord rescued me. Indeed, all who desire to live a godly life in Christ Jesus will be persecuted, while evil people and impostors will go on from bad to worse, deceiving and being deceived. But as for you, continue in what you have learned and have firmly believed, knowing from whom you learned it and how

> from childhood you have been acquainted with the sacred writings, which are able to make you wise for salvation through faith in Christ Jesus.

Paul began the paragraph with the word "δε" which is translated as the coordinating conjunction "but." This indicates a contrast between what the apostle had previously written within the immediate context and what he was about to say regarding godly leadership. What Paul stated in 2 Timothy 3:1–9 (ESV) was that immediately prior to the return of Christ there would be perilous times characterized by perilous people.

> For people will be lovers of self, lovers of money, proud, arrogant, abusive, disobedient to their parents, ungrateful, unholy, heartless, unappeasable, slanderous, without self-control, brutal, not loving good, treacherous, reckless, swollen with conceit, lovers of pleasure rather than lovers of God, having the appearance of godliness, but denying its power. Avoid such people. (2 Timothy 3:2–5, ESV)

Commentator William Hendrickson writes:

> Accordingly, Paul's words here in 2 Timothy 3:1 are best interpreted as meaning, Timothy, constantly realize that in these last days—this lengthy dispensation—*in which we are now living* there will be grievous seasons. These seasons will come and go, and the last will be worse than the first. They will be seasons of ever-increasing wickedness, which will culminate in the climax of wickedness. (Hendrickson, 282–283)

Paul commented that these individuals would also "oppose the truth, men corrupted in mind and disqualified regarding the faith" (2 Timothy 3:8, ESV). However, the apostle indicated that they would not progress in influence but rather their "folly will be plain to all" (2 Timothy 3:9, ESV).

What kind of godly leaders should Christians be in the midst of increasing ungodliness and conflict? Paul does not leave his young son guessing nor later readers for that matter. The apostle encourages leaders to realize several things about being a godly leader in the midst of conflict.

First, they are to remember Paul's example. They are to "carefully follow" the apostle's life and ministry. This means to "investigate carefully and to follow what has been grasped" (Kittel, 34). What areas of Paul's life and ministry are open to personal examination and investigation? Paul lists nine items for scrutiny: the doctrine, the manner of life, the purpose, the faith, the longsuffering, the love, the perseverance, the persecutions, and the afflictions. It is noted that in the Greek text the definite article prefaces each of the items. What do these categories mean?

- Doctrine. This is "διδασκαλια" (*didaskalia),* which means teaching. What a leader communicates. It is what a pastor preaches.
- Manner of life. This is from the word "αγωγη" (*agōgē).* It means conduct or behavior. It refers to a consecrated walk of life (1 Corinthians 4:17, ESV). A leader is to demonstrate unselfishness in his life wherein he strives to give God all the glory.
- Purpose. "προθεσει" (*prothesis, prosthesis)* means God's purposes. The goal of the leader's life is in total harmony with his teaching. There is no contradiction and no hypocrisy.

- Faith. "πιστει" (*pistis)* in the context means Paul's personal faith in God.
- Longsuffering. This is from the word "μακροθυμια" (*makrothymia)* meaning patience
- Love. "αγαπη" (*agape)* means self-sacrificial love of the will.
- Perseverance. "Υπομονη" (*hypomonē)* means endurance under pressure. When life's conflicts are the toughest, the godly leader perseveres.
- Persecutions. "διωγμοις" (*diōgmos)* refers to what Paul passively endured.
- Afflictions. This is "παθημασιν" (*pathēma)* and means to suffer. These sufferings were for the cause of Christ and are recounted in 2 Corinthians 11:21–33 (ESV). Paul refers to what he suffered at Antioch, Iconium, and Lystra in verse11.

Paul's encouragement to godly leaders is that since as he demonstrated holy living and endured a variety of conflict, so should they. They should expect conflict, grow from conflict, and always emulate godliness and a commitment to biblical truth throughout conflict.

Second, leaders are to remember Christ's faithfulness. Christ delivered Paul from all of his persecutions and afflictions. This truth of God's deliverance reverberates throughout the Scriptures. See Psalm 34:4–6, 19 (ESV); Psalm 37:40 (ESV); Psalm 91:2–6 (ESV); Isaiah 41:10 (ESV); Isaiah 43:2 (ESV); Daniel 3:17 (ESV); Acts 26:16–17 (ESV); and 2 Corinthians 1:10 (ESV). It should be an encouragement to godly leaders today.

Third, leaders are to realize that conflict will occur. The apostle stated that "Indeed, all who desire to live a godly life in Christ Jesus will be persecuted" (2 Timothy 3:12, ESV). Conflict is going to happen. God is providentially stating such is the case. The context dictates that this persecution will come from the Christ-rejecting world, but they should expect that conflict will also come from within the church. Therefore, believers must expect it and determine to be godly leaders when it occurs.

Fourth, conflict is not going to get any easier. Paul states that "evil people and impostors will go on from bad to worse, deceiving and being deceived" (2 Timothy 3:13, ESV). Evil, from "πονηροι " (*ponēros)*, contains the sense of "bad, harmful, unserviceable, or useless" (Kittel, 913). In the moral sense, and used as an adjective, "evil" refers to humans who contrast God's holiness (Matthew 10:18, ESV), who are morally reprehensible (Matthew 7:11, ESV), and ultimately oppose God (Matthew 12:34–35, ESV).

The word imposters, "γοητες" (*goēs)*, means magician. In the context of 2 Timothy, it "can denote any charlatan referring to the confusion and delusion of idolatry or hypocritical or sensual conduct. The only New Testament usage is in 2 Timothy 3:13, where the sense is the figurative one for the person who entices others to impious actions by pious words" (Kittel, 126).

Paul is telling godly leaders that evil men and imposters are a reality and they will continue to grow worse and worse. They not only will continue to deceive but will also continue to be deceived. Their deception, both given and received, finds its source in Satan. The godly leader must realize that he will encounter conflict in ministry. There is no discontinuance from the conflict God sovereignly permits in the ministry where He has called the godly leader to serve.

Fifth, godly leaders are to remain faithful. Godly leaders must continue in the things they have learned and from whom they have learned them. Principles gleaned and examples evidenced from the Scriptures and experiences must never be forgotten. Godly leaders must remember their heritage.

The Lord continues to challenge me with the fact that God-ordained conflict is indispensable in developing godly leadership qualities in me. Conflict is a fact of life in the ministry and for a leader. It seems occasionally to rear its head when you least expect it. However, the question is never will there be conflict, but rather, how will I handle conflict when it comes and what type of godly leader am I, not only in the midst of the conflict but also in its aftermath?

William Cowper (1731–1800) was no stranger to conflict and trials. He battled depression throughout his life and even lived for a period of time in an insane asylum. However, his poetry reflects God's sustaining character and grace. I submit one of Cowper's most familiar hymns as an encouragement to godly leaders encountering the refining fires of conflict.

God moves in a mysterious way
His wonders to perform;
He plants His footsteps in the sea,
And rides upon the storm.

"Great privilege! Great pain! God's design! This is God's way: to take the privilege of faith and strengthen it with trials so that we worship and witness with a greater passion for God" (Piper, 179).

May every leader's legacy be of counting it all joy in the midst of trials and finding God's grace to be sufficient. *Soli Deo Gloria!*

BIBLIOGRAPHY

Adamson, James. The New International Commentary on the New Testament: *The Epistle of James.* Grand Rapids: Eerdmans, 1976.

"Adversity." Harris. R; Laird, Gleason L. Archer Jr., and Bruce K. Waltke, eds. *Theological Workbook of the Old Testament.* Chicago: Moody, 1980.

Alongside Cares. http://www.aongsidecares.net.

Bartlett's Familiar Quotations. 10th Edition. http://www.bartleby.com/html.

Biblical Conflict Resolution. http://www.biblicalresources.info/pages/pastoral/ Conflicts/conflict.

Bridges, Jerry. *Transforming Grace: Living Confidently in God's Unfailing Love.* Colorado Springs: Navpress, 1991.

Calvin, John. *Calvin's New Testament Commentaries, vol. 10. The Second Epistle of Paul the Apostle to the Corinthians and the Epistles to Timothy, Titus and Philemon.* David Torrance and Thomas F. Torrance, Eds. Grand Rapids: Eerdmans, 1985.

"Conflict." *Oxford Illustrated American Dictionary.* 1988 ed.

"Conflict." Gerhard Kittle, and Gerhard Friedrich, eds. *Theological Dictionary of the New Testament.* Grand Rapids: Eerdmans, 1985.

"Contend." Gerhard Kittle, and Gerhard Friedrich, eds. *Theological Dictionary of the New Testament.* Grand Rapids: Eerdmans, 1985.

Cowper, William. "God Moves in a Mysterious Way." *The Poetical Words of William Cowper.* Ed. William Michael Rossetti. Chicago: Rand McNally, 1902.

"Discipline." *Oxford Illustrated American Dictionary.* 1988 ed.

"Discipline." Gerhard Kittle, and Gerhard Friedrich, eds. *Theological Dictionary of the New Testament.* Grand Rapids: Eerdmans, 1985.

"Earthly." Gerhard Kittle, and Gerhard Friedrich, eds. *Theological Dictionary of the New Testament.* Grand Rapids: Eerdmans, 1985.

Ellis, Joseph J. *His Excellency George Washington.* New York: Knopf, 2004.

"Evil." Gerhard Kittle, and Gerhard Friedrich, eds. *Theological Dictionary of the New Testament.* Grand Rapids: Eerdmans, 1985.

"Excellent Spirit." Harris. R; Laird, Gleason L. Archer Jr., and Bruce K. Waltke, eds. *Theological Workbook of the Old Testament.* Chicago: Moody, 1980.

"Fear." Harris. R; Laird, Gleason L. Archer Jr., and Bruce K. Waltke, eds. *Theological Workbook of the Old Testament.* Chicago: Moody, 1980.

Ferguson, Sinclair. *John Owen on the Christian Life.* Edinburgh: Banner, 1995.

———. *Mastering the Old Testament: Daniel.* Ed. Lloyd J. Ogilvie. Dallas: Word, 1988.

"Forsook." *Strong's Exhaustive Concordance.* James Strong, ed. Nashville: Regal, 1985.

Gromacki, Robert G. *New Testament Survey.* Grand Rapids: Baker, 1974.

"Heart." Gerhard Kittle, and Gerhard Friedrich, eds. *Theological Dictionary of the New Testament.* Grand Rapids: Eerdmans, 1985.

"Heart." W.E. Vine, ed. *An Expository Dictionary of New Testament Words.* Nashville: Nelson, 1996.

Hendricks, Howard. *Cameos of Character.* National Leadership Conference. Dallas Theological Seminary. Dallas. 19-22 Oct. 1999.

Hendrickson, William. *New Testament Commentary: Galatians and Ephesians.* Grand Rapids: Baker, 1979.

——— *New Testament Commentary: Romans.* Grand Rapids: Baker, 1981.

Hughes, Phillip E. *A Commentary on the Epistle to the Hebrews.* Grand Rapids: Eerdmans, 1977.

"Integrity." *Oxford Illustrated American Dictionary. 1988 ed.*

LaSor, William S., David Allen Hubbard, and Fredrick William Bush. *Old Testament Survey.* Grand Rapids: Eerdmans, 1982.

"Job." Harris. R; Laird, Gleason L. Archer Jr., and Bruce K. Waltke, eds. *Theological Workbook of the Old Testament.* Chicago: Moody, 1980.

"Joy." *Oxford Illustrated American Dictionary.* 1988 ed.

"Joy." Gerhard Kittle, and Gerhard Friedrich, eds. *Theological Dictionary of the New Testament.* Grand Rapids: Eerdmans, 1985.

MacArthur, John. *An Uncompromising Life.* Chicago: Moody, 1988.

Manchester, William. *The Last Lion: Winston Spencer Churchill: Visions of Glory1874-1932.* Little, Brown and Company; 1st edition, 1983.

"Memorial." Harris. R; Laird, Gleason L. Archer Jr., and Bruce K. Waltke, eds. *Theological Workbook of the Old Testament.* Chicago: Moody, 1980.

Michael, Larry. *Spurgeon on Leadership.* Grand Rapids: Kregel, 2003.

"Mighty." Harris. R; Laird, Gleason L. Archer Jr., and Bruce K. Waltke, eds. *Theological Workbook of the Old Testament.* Chicago: Moody, 1980.

Moo, Douglas. *James.* Tyndale New Testament Commentaries. Ed. Leon Morris. Grand Rapids: Eerdmans, 1985.

Murray, Iain. Jonathan Edwards: *A New Biography.* Edinburgh: Banner of Truth Trust, 1987.

Narramore, Clyde M. *Why a Christian Leader May Fall.* Crossway, 1988.

Packer, James I. *Knowing God.* Downers Grove: Intervarsity, 1993.

"Patience." Gerhard Kittle, and Gerhard Friedrich, eds. *Theological Dictionary of the New Testament.* Grand Rapids: Eerdmans, 1985.

Piper, John. *The Hidden Smile of God: The Fruit of Affliction in the Loves of John Bunyan, William Cowper, and David Brainerd.* Wheaton: Crossway, 2001.

"Progress." Gerhard Kittle, and Gerhard Friedrich, eds. *Theological Dictionary of the New Testament.* Grand Rapids: Eerdmans, 1985.

Shaara, Jeff. *The Glorious Cause.* New York: Ballentine, 2002.

Swindoll, Charles R., *Daniel: God's Pattern for the Future.* Anaheim: Insight, 1996.

—-. *The Heart of a Great Leader.* Clergy Conference. Promise Keepers.

"Thronged." *Strong's Exhaustive Concordance.* James Strong, ed. Nashville: Regal, 1985.

"Tumult." *Oxford Illustrated American Dictionary.* 1988 ed.

"Tumult." Harris. R; Laird, Gleason L. Archer Jr., and Bruce K. Waltke, eds. *Theological Workbook of the Old Testament.* Chicago: Moody, 1980.

Willmington, Harold L. *Willmington's Guide to the Bible.* Wheaton: Tyndale, 1982.

"Various." Gerhard Kittle, and Gerhard Friedrich, eds. *Theological Dictionary of the New Testament.* Grand Rapids: Eerdmans, 1985.

Wood, Leon. *A Commentary on Daniel.* Grand Rapids: Zondervan, 1973.

"Young Men." Harris. R; Laird, Gleason L. Archer Jr., and Bruce K. Waltke, eds. *Theological Workbook of the Old Testament.* Chicago: Moody, 1980.